"Reading this book stirred the m
Me the Old, Old Story. Joel mas
powerful, life-changing ways by c
provides seven strategic questions to help the reader do heart (crawlspace) surgery. It is a great read for any Christian. It is an exceptional homework assignment for every counselee. You will laugh, you will shed a few tears, and you will identify. You will be spiritually challenged. In its simplicity, it is powerful."

Howard Eyrich, MA. ThM. DMin.
Director of the Doctor of Ministry/Counseling
Birmingham Theological Seminary.
Author of multiple books including *Curing the Heart: A Model for Biblical Counseling* (2002) with co-author William Hines.

"I, yet again, envy Joel's mind and ability to breakdown big concepts. This book cuts through a world of chaotic info and delivers clear, concise practical challenge. Strong mental health requires good mental workouts and this book is like hitting the mental gym!"

Junior Ziegler, author of
The Vitals: The Critical Organs of Christianity (2012)
The {Man}ual: A Practical Guide to Manhood (2023)

"There are a couple of million reasons to check out Joel's *The Crawlspace of the Heart*, but I'll try to narrow them down to a few. Joel never pretends to be perfect, to having it all figured out. He isn't oblivious to the reality of the challenges we face (whether we care to admit them or not). He doesn't pretend that we are not still affected on some level by sin, struggle, and suffering. What Joel does is direct us towards the one who can make the difference - Jesus. And this not just for Christians. It is written for anyone who is tired of a life on a bad repeat. 'Life sometimes really stinks, but God is always faithful!' Things can and do get better when you go to the right person and address the problem at the crawlspace of the heart."

Mick Duran, teacher, scholar, and friend.

"Joel has been our family pastor for over 15 years. So when he told me he was writing a book, I looked forward to reading it. I was not disappointed. His book shows him as the care pastor that he is. I highly recommend his book. As his friendship has, his book has increased me. A great read."

Terry Johnson, long-time friend and former church elder.

The Crawlspace of the Heart

Seven Questions To Reveal Your Deepest Issues

By JOEL M. BRADSHAW

2024, Big Rev Publishing

Chicago, IL

All rights reserved.

ISBN: 9798323910342

All Bible quotations contained in this book, unless otherwise noted, are from the English Standard Version translation. The Holy Bible, English Standard Version® (ESV®) © 2001 by Crossway, a publishing ministry of Good News Publishers. All rights reserved.

CONTENTS

DEDICATION

I dedicate this book to my wonderful wife, Jennifer. Jen, God has used you tremendously in my life to encourage me to be more like Jesus. You helped me to bravely face my own issues and be intentional about the right things in my life. I love you so much!

To my son Joshua and daughter Julia, I am also thankful for you and grateful to be your Dad. As you grow, I pray you learn to trust Jesus during difficult seasons. I hope one of our family legacies will be to carry with you biblical questions like the ones in this book. I love you and am proud of you!

A WORD BEFORE WE BEGIN

I am a certified biblical counselor, but I don't intend this book as a replacement for biblical counseling. I actually think that what is contained in these chapters provides great introductory work for your biblical mental health journey. I encourage you to use what you discover about yourself as foundational work moving forward. This book contains questions in each chapter. Please write your answers in this book. Most of the questions contained here are ones I not only ask myself but also ask the counselees I journey with.

The good news is that Jesus is the hero of your recovery, and His Word, the Bible, is what works in you. The Bible verses in these chapters challenge and encourage me in my own journey. Thank you for purchasing this book and for investigating the "crawlspace"'of your heart!

All for the glory of God! (1 Corinthians 10:31)

PREFACE

Many years ago, my wife and I had a chaotic moment in the kitchen that ended up changing the way I look at life and ministry. We were hanging out together at the kitchen table doing a jigsaw puzzle and we started seeing little flying insects everywhere.

I remember Jennifer asking me what they were. I thought that maybe we had left fruit out somewhere, and had started looking behind the toaster and the microwave. But these weren't fruit flies. They were gnats. We couldn't believe it.

So I grabbed a flyswatter and Jen some bug spray. And for five coordinated minutes we exercised great teamwork. Even though we thought our dedicated efforts had solved the problem, we began to notice that the gnats kept coming. Soon, we discovered them flying in from the landing between the basement stairs and the kitchen. They were invading from the basement!

Now, we had taken on floodwater a few times living in that house, so we figured something else had at one point gone wrong. We thus turned on the basement lights and began searching for movement. When we reached the laundry room and switched on the fluorescents, we discovered them—hundreds and hundreds of gnats!

Well, we immediately resumed our routine. I again swatted and she sprayed. Soon, we had dead gnats all over the walls and lights. We were so frustrated that we even decided to leave the corpses behind in case others came back. Little did we know.

About two gnat-free weeks later, we found ourselves sitting in the kitchen again. This time, Jen was beating me in a game of Scrabble. Gnats! We wasted no time in heading to the basement and into the laundry room. Hundreds and hundreds of gnats once again covered the walls and ceiling lights. The corpses we left behind had not deterred them. For a third time, I swatted and Jen sprayed. It was getting disgusting down there. But, we were making a point. Evidently, we were also missing one.
Two weeks later, a fourth round of gnats invaded. We charged into the laundry room and then frustratingly started looking around. Something had to give. Was there some uneaten sandwich down there? Had the dog left a surprise or two in a corner? Then Jen noticed that the gnats were surrounding the area behind the dryer.

So I pulled the dryer out and we saw a door! We hadn't really ever noticed a door there before. And of course, a bunch of gnats were surrounding the space by the door where the dryer had rested.

We opened the door and noticed a great dark area that seemed to span the length of the upstairs. I shined a flashlight into the area, but could only make out things like the sump pump and pipes in the ceiling. Mercifully, there was a little light switch chain. I pulled it and saw a whole new world down there. Yes, it was the crawlspace for the house.

We called one of the church trustees, and he came over and investigated the crawlspace. And I was thankful. I had played a year of college football as a nose tackle. And my large frame was not easily fitting through that door or hunched down in

that space. My smaller and more handy friend crawled in the little doorway and within two minutes had diagnosed the problem.
There was a pipe that traveled from the kitchen to the drainage area, and it had evidently rotted through. As my friend described it, in the pea gravel below the pipe there was a mound of smelly waste and on top of that mound were thousands of gnats.

Now, I was the church pastor living in that parsonage. It was our first house experience and I had no idea how to fix anything. Any time I had a housing issue one of the church trustees had come to my rescue! Thankfully, my buddy had a plumber friend who happened to have a spare copper pipe. With the fresh pipe installed, my friend the trustee painfully crawled into the area and filled up large, orange buckets with the horrible mess and later poured fresh pea gravel. We never had another gnat.

So what was the problem? You see, the dishwasher wasn't in the best shape, so my wife and I had washed dishes by hand every night. What we didn't know was that with every load of dishes, food particles were going down the drain, out of the broken pipe, and depositing themselves in the gravel. We were unknowingly constantly feeding the gnats!

Getting into that crawlspace was hard and sometimes painful. I am thankful for my friend, and for his friend, and the help they provided. I am thankful for my wife noticing the door. I have used this illustration many times as I journey with hurting people.

You see, had we not done the hard work of getting into the crawlspace, we would have just kept swatting gnats. The source of the issue would never have been addressed, the solution never found, and the frustrations would have increasingly mounted. We might have not even hired someone to help, because we were seemingly solving our problem in the short-term.

It's been my story that the issues we face in life flow from the heart. And as I lead men and women to seek the Bible for answers to their problems, I invite them to investigate the crawlspace of their hearts. To see what things are revealed when the lights are turned on. To take steps to not only humbly face issues, but turn to God for hope and help.

In twenty years of pastoral ministry, I have found seven basic questions that have helped to uncover the deepest problems of the heart. These are the seven chapters of this book. Biblical counseling causes us to look into the crawlspaces of our hearts. We are invited to do necessary, but hard, work and to trust God with the results.

I thank you for making it this far. If you can answer these seven questions, you will reveal your "crawlspace" issues. The journey might seem challenging and even painful at times. But, it beats swatting gnats.

CHAPTER 1

WHAT DO YOU REALLY WANT?

It was day 3 of the biblical counseling conference in Lafayette, Indiana. I was hours away from my family and was learning material at such a pace that it felt like taking a sip from a firehose. Then the conference speaker dropped this line:

I DO WHAT I DO, BECAUSE I WANT WHAT I WANT.[1]

It was one of those moments that changed my life. I remember sitting in my seat with my conference notebook in my lap and feverishly taking notes—only to stop. That very line cut to the core of my heart. My eyes had gotten big and my mouth had dropped open a bit. I remember thinking WOW. I might have even softly said it. I immediately filled the margin of my notebook with the pivotal phrase.

It's just a great line. And it can easily be augmented various ways. I remember the speaker leading us through this thought exercise. Just substitute some part of your life for the word

---

[1] Aucoin, Brent. "Understanding the Heart." 2019 Biblical Counseling Training Conference: Track 1. Faith Biblical Counseling Ministry of Faith Church of Lafayette, IN. (February 11, 2019)

"do" in the first part of the sentence. I say what I say, because I want what I want. I think what I think, because I want what I want. I feel how I feel. I am how I am. And the best part about statements like these is that they invite a key question.

<u>What do you really want?</u>

That question digs down to the deepest levels of the inside person revealing the very seat of motivations. It uncovers hidden excuses and rationalizations that provide fodder to feed the narratives we tell ourselves as we don't reach the goals we pursue. Did you catch that? When I personally don't reach a goal, I go looking for a story to tell. That story is found within excuses and rationalizations I am thus tempted to hold. If I can tell a story and will get you to agree with that story, then I am, in my mind, momentarily let off the hook for not staying diligent towards the goal.

I know that has been my story regarding my weight loss journey. What do I want? I often would tell myself and others that I wanted to lose weight. So the question needs to be immediately asked what I did about it. Because if I really wanted to lose weight, I would have proceeded to make the daily choices necessary to pursue that goal. When I chose not to catalogue my food intake or go to the gym, those were decisions that revealed that I really wanted something different.

So what might I have wanted more than losing weight? I think I wanted to not really be burdened. I wanted to have the goal and to be seen by others as pursuing the goal, but I didn't want to do the hard work to attain it. <u>I wanted change, but didn't want to change.</u> I thus resisted discipline, because discipline is difficult. It was far easier to say that I wanted to lose weight than it was to be diligent and stay disciplined. I did what I did, because I wanted what I wanted. If I truly wanted to lose weight, I would have made different choices.

My weight loss journey has thus historically ebbed and flowed. The hardest part for me was always starting over. I would have lost a bunch of weight and then progressively over the months and years gained much of it back. Then, for whatever reason, I was convicted again to lose the weight. So I had to face the shameful realization in my story that I had lost the weight before and gained it back. I would have to cross much of the same territory I had already traveled. I would then ponder what was I doing with my life. Was I not being intentional? What would others think of my journey?

So I would craft the excuses. I had suffered a difficult season of grief. I journeyed with depression and therefore had endured a difficult year emotionally. And I wouldn't have to say too much before my audience would agree with me and wonder how I was even sitting up and taking nourishment after all! When I endured my difficult season of life I usually self-medicated with a bag of chips rather than a bottle of alcohol. I therefore thought I needed to escape my pain.

That was the narrative I not only told myself but also others. It also revealed another key want: I wanted people to agree with my story and let me off the hook for failing to stay diligent. This especially worked because when people heard my story they were quick to care for me. In a sense, they gave me what I wanted which were that my excuses would indeed be excused! When we use excuses and rationalizations that way we are being persuasive towards our audience. We desire our "want" to be approved so that we can feel justified in not doing what we should have done. I wanted other things more than I wanted to lose weight and my back and forth journey illustrated that.

I do what I do, because I want what I want. Your story may not be weight loss. However, you do want something and your daily choices reveal what you indeed want most. With that in mind, I'd like to biblically lead you through four questions. I know, this chapter is already a question, but I've found that questions that lead to further questions are helpful. So let's ask four questions and investigate how the Bible directs our answers.

What do you do?

It doesn't make much sense to ask what you want until you face what you do. This will be a brave journey for you to undertake. I challenge you to be bold with yourself in your honesty. If you are like me, you will be writing things down to which you might feel embarrassment, guilt, or even shame. When I was supposed to be on my diet, I would always hide my fast food value meals and eat by myself. Here, we are not hiding. Let's take the opportunity to prayerfully make a list. This is your book. Go ahead and write in the blank spaces. If you need other space or would rather not mark in your book, then write the questions down elsewhere.

"God, I pray for the one reading this right now who is possibly facing him or herself for the first time. Reveal what they need to write down and give them the strength to do so. I pray this in Jesus' Name, Amen."

The things you do only in front of other people:

The things you do when nobody else is around:

The attitudes you maintain that accompany your words and actions:

The things you do and find yourself making excuses about:

The things you self-justify or try to get others to agree with you on to maintain your story:

The words you intentionally choose to say:

Thank you for doing that. Facing yourself is always one of the bravest things you could do. I'm proud of you and your honesty. I'm sure you noticed that the questions were in the present tense. There is a value in analyzing your past.[2] For my purposes here, I find it more helpful to ask about the things you are currently doing, rather than what you have previously done. We will analyze your story and your past later. So let's keep the context present and current.

This chapter aims to discover what you really want, not what you historically have wanted. Although, it would not take much for you to analyze your answers through the lens of your historical journey. I doubt what you have done and what you have wanted have changed that much.
Can I introduce you to someone you probably already know? You know him as a theological stalwart, but he also faced himself and the things he did. His name is Paul. You might have referred to him before as the Apostle Paul.

For I do not understand my own actions. For I do not do what I want, but I do the very thing I hate. Now if I do what I do not want, I agree with the law, that it is good. So now it is no longer I who do it, but sin that dwells within me. For I know that nothing good dwells in me, that is, in my flesh. For I have the desire to do what is right, but not the ability to carry it out. For I do not do the good I want, but the evil I do not want is what I keep on doing. (Romans 7:15-19)

Just look at that struggle. He wants to do what is right, but still does what is wrong. Many of us who are caught in those habitual sins hate them. We loathe the fact that we keep doing them. But we also at some level still want to do them. And we can't stand that we live both sides of the struggle. Paul is so relatable here. Paul was making a larger point about being a slave to sin and sin working in his life, but the struggle was still genuine. And since Paul struggled with what he wanted and what he ended up doing, be encouraged that the path you are on is a good one. Stay focused and let's keep asking questions.

---

[2] Viars, Stephen. *Putting Your Past in Its Place: Moving Forward in Freedom and Forgiveness.* (Harvest House Publishers, 2011). Eugene, OR.

What do you want?

At this point, it makes sense to look at the things you are doing. You just took all that time and intentionally made your lists. What do the things you are actually doing reveal about your heart? My weight loss choices revealed that I really wanted something different than losing weight. What does what you do reveal about you at your core? I invite you to dig deep. Most likely the thing you want most is self-pursuing. You want to feel peace. You want security. You want comfort, etc.

Maybe you are like me (and like Paul!) and actually want to honor God with your life, but you struggle. Let's return to Romans but one chapter later and take a look at a perspective that has helped me as I answered this question.

For those who live according to the flesh set their minds on the things of the flesh, but those who live according to the Spirit set their minds on the things of the Spirit. For to set the mind on the flesh is death, but to set the mind on the Spirit is life and peace. For the mind that is set on the flesh is hostile to God, for it does not submit to God's law; indeed, it cannot. Those who are in the flesh cannot please God. (Romans 8:5-8)

This is the great dichotomy—you live either to please God or to please yourself. You thus pursue the things of the flesh or the things of God. The things of the flesh are temporal and self-oriented. The things of God are ultimately eternal and centered around Him. In your life, you might be balancing an intentional both/and with regards to your wants. But our text today doesn't describe a both/and but rather an either/or. At some point in the heart the either/or is revealed. You do what you do, because you want what you want.

So what do you truly at your core want? Have you set your mind more on yourself or on God? Who do you picture as your greatest want, a version of yourself or Jesus? For the Christian reading this, the previous sentence is worth reading a few times more. At your core, you have an either/or and not a both/and. Or if you have a both/and, it's threatening to become an either/or. Jesus famously preached that you can't serve two masters. He was speaking of career/money and God (Matthew 6:24).

You do what you do, because you want what you want. You therefore set your mind where you have because you want what you want. The Romans passage above presents one of two choices. Your choices may be different than those, but they still will resolve in one being the most important. Theologically speaking, you are either pursuing God or yourself. Look at your list of the things you do again. What are they communicating about your heart? Of those choices please list what you want most.

Now take a moment and look at what you just wrote down. Is there a want that is actually deeper? You might have listed something on the first floor of your building, but there is a foundational want on which you should focus. The wife who wrote down, "I want my husband to listen to me" might actually be wanting to be seen as important or valued at a more foundational level and longs for her husband to affirm her. And digging deeper, she might want others to agree with her and her story. She might want approval most. She might want to actually matter and she therefore sees others as providing this for her. Think for a bit about revisiting what you wrote down. Has it changed? Keep doing this until you get to the basement level of your building.

Are your wants representative of a both/and or an either/or? Focus on the either/or now. This will help you isolate what you want most at your core.

What should you do?

By this point, you've stated what you do and have begun to analyze underneath what you truly want. If you are serious about lasting change in your life, you will continue to ask the question of what you want. That's why this is the opening chapter of this book. Knowing your true motivation in life is essential at getting to the crawlspace of your heart.

But for change to truly happen, I recommend asking the questions with a new focus. When we bring should into our questions we imply standards and make judgment calls regarding our adherence to those standards. In terms of theology, when I ask should questions, it brings God into my story.

<u>The heart that looks for excuses is different than the heart that looks for discipline.</u> Ponder for a moment a chief goal of the Old Testament:

You shall love the LORD your God with all your heart and with all your soul and with all your might. (Deuteronomy 6:5)

That word "all" sticks in the craw just a bit, doesn't it? Moses wasn't commanding the Israelites to love God with some of their hearts, but all. So the verse invites us to take a look at what we actually do and then sift it through the expectation of what we should do. I do what I do, because I want what I want. So either I read a verse like Deuteronomy 6:5 and seek excuses or pursue discipline. This is why Israel needed the reminder of the verses that follow:

And these words that I command you today shall be on your heart. You shall teach them diligently to your children, and shall talk of them when you sit in your house, and when you walk by the way, and when you lie down, and when you rise. You shall bind them as a sign on your hand, and they shall be as frontlets between your eyes. You shall write them on the doorposts of your house and on your gates. (Deuteronomy 6:6-9)

<u>Discipline is an every day thing and an everywhere thing.</u> A man once asked Jesus about what he thought was the greatest of the commandments.

And [Jesus] said to him, "You shall love the Lord your God with all your heart and with all your soul and with all your mind. This is the great and first commandment. And a second is like it: You shall love your neighbor as yourself. On these two commandments depend all the Law and the Prophets." (Matthew 22:37-40)

Jesus added Leviticus 19:18 to Deuteronomy 6. But his point was clear: loving God and loving neighbor summarizes what a person should do.

Let's revisit our responses from question 1. Based upon the testimony from Moses and Jesus, we have ultimate answers to these questions. So I invite you to answer them a second time, but now with the framework of loving God and loving others. How do those verses change your answers?

The things you do only in front of other people:

The things you do when nobody else is around:

The attitudes you maintain that accompany your words and actions:

The things you do and find yourself making excuses about:

Things you self-justify or try to get others to agree with you on to maintain your story:

The words you intentionally choose to say:

Were your answers different from before? How did they change? Knowing that God expects me to act a certain way is both comforting and convicting. Comforting in that I don't have to search for the purpose of life anymore. Convicting because I often fail short of the standards that God expects of me.

What should you want?

I have been recently journeying in the Psalms. And while in Psalm 86, a verse stood out to me that perfectly describes the answer to this question.

Teach me your way, O LORD, that I may walk in your truth; unite my heart to fear your name. (Psalm 86:11)

<u>Good leaders are also good submitters.</u> And David wanted to be led by God. In fact, David prayed here in a way that would be more commonly acted out in Jesus' day. Advanced students would apply to a rabbi and ask him to teach his purposes and ways to them and to be able to follow as disciples. David wanted to know God's path and then wanted to walk that path. This is a good perspective to have.

A number of years ago, I gave a teaching at our local Celebrate Recovery group and I shared about God's faithfulness in my life leading me to many years of sobriety regarding my once-addictive behaviors. In the area I most struggled, God had grown in me discipline in the place of selfishness. Later, a younger man came up to me and said almost exactly David's words in the above verse. He wanted me to teach him what I did for he wanted what I had. Over the next couple of years, I discipled this man and prayed with him and for him.

More recently, an atheist friend of mine who struggles maintaining sobriety also asked me to teach him what I learned in my journey. When I mentioned that this would involve me speaking about Jesus, he assured me that he wouldn't take offense. He simply wanted to learn about the discipline I found!

David next prayed that God would unite his heart and David would use that undivided heart to fully fear God. He wanted internal unity as if there were two warring desires within him. We have those same two desires at war within us: a desire for the self and a desire for God. On our own, we will never choose God and will always choose the self. Any choice of ours that prioritizes God over self originates in God's work within us. That's the story of my life and your life. Sin and selfishness are otherwise too pervasive, too powerful.[3]

David prayed that God would work within him so that he would be able to respond to God. David needed a heart that wasn't divided. He needed his motivations and decision-making processes to be joined with God. He longed for unity where there was division. He was a man after God's heart, because he wanted a heart like God's. He was therefore a leader that wanted to be led. David was a man who wanted his submission to God to not be laced with hypocrisy. He feared God too much to want otherwise.

Does that describe you or do you delight in your little, secretly-divided heart? What should you want? You should want to be led by God's word, and then to live a life that obeys that biblical teaching. <u>Your united heart is motivated by a healthy fear of God, not to see what you can get away with in your journey.</u>

---

3 Sproul, R.C. "TULIP and Reformed Theology: Total Depravity", https://www.ligonier.org/learn/articles/tulip-and-reformed-theology-total-depravity, (Accessed November 15, 2023).

I know this is a struggle for me. What I should do and what I actually do are often at odds with each other. So it is with what I should want and what I actually want. Are you the same way? What about your desires needs to change to align with what God wants? What did you write down in this chapter as your chief desire?

Does the Bible address that desire? If so, does it reveal that desire as honoring God most or yourself? Is it a desire to love God and to love neighbor? Should you be desiring this or does it reveal that you are divided between yourself and God? Is there a better, or at least a more biblical, desire that you should have at your core?

Please take a moment and add any thoughts to where your journey has led you in this chapter.

My daily choices reveal what I prioritize and yours do as well. Some people complain that they never have time to read their Bible or to pray. And yet, they are always current on the shows that they stream. Think of the thing in your life you would never miss doing if you could help it.

When I lived I Wisconsin, I journeyed with people who would never miss a Packers game. In Illinois, they would never miss the Bears. Life got rearranged for when kickoff was scheduled. Church attendance would be massaged. Other activities would not even make the calendar. They wanted to watch the game and so they did what was necessary to make it happen. I would sometimes be informed that their team was "the early game" that day on the TV schedule. So make sure the sermon doesn't go too long, Pastor! There was a twinkle in the eye when they said those words, but I knew they contained fire behind them. I even recall having church event participation skipped because of the playoffs. Even when their team wasn't in the postseason! They did what they did, because they wanted what they wanted.

I recall a season when I would say I wanted to be a better husband, but wouldn't do the Ephesians 5:25 work necessary to make it a priority. I remember once or twice feeling convicted and making great pronouncements regarding my purity journey, but wouldn't take advantage of accountability relationships and helpful computer software. Discipline is fun when other people start noticing you are putting in the work and seeing some results. But eventually the opinions of other people cease to motivate. The heart has to be engaged. <u>Your choices will reveal your priorities.</u> You do what you do, because you want what you want.

This was a tough chapter to write. It reminded me that I still have plenty of work to do regarding my own choices. It might have been a difficult chapter to read. We often say we want different things in life, but if we are unwilling to make the appropriate, disciplined choices that are necessary, then we won't see those changes.

Imagine you were a friend of mine during my weight loss accordion-style back and forth journey. You might have asked me some tougher questions. If we were close then you might have even risked hurting me to ask them. For you saw my health as more important than my feelings. Think of this chapter with that in mind. I've asked some tougher questions. I've encouraged you to bravely face the reality of yourself. And to your credit, you put pen to paper and recorded what you do and what you desire most. You even brought the Bible to your situation and pondered what you should do and should desire.

I'm proud of you. You've made it this far. The crawlspace of your heart has gotten one question clearer. If you are willing to journey with me further, please turn the page. For question two is just as important as question one.

CHAPTER 2

WHAT DO YOU TELL YOURSELF MOST?

The vast majority of people that have found their way into conversations with me have been depressed. I read it in their prayer requests. I see it in their eyes. I hear it in their voices. The horrible "best friend" of depression is shame. It's usually the shame that I hear first. This is when the story transitions from "I did something horrible" to "I am something horrible."[4]

Depression is the mood response when something has been in your crawlspace for far too long. The usual culprits are grief, hurt, rejection, and guilt. So I begin to ask questions. What is the underlying source of your sadness? How have you been hurt? What happened in your past? Do you feel guilty about something?

I have faced depression for most of my adult life. It all started from my childhood weight struggles. I was usually the heaviest

---

4 "Shame is a focus on self, guilt is a focus on behavior. Shame is "I am bad." Guilt is "I did something bad." Taken from a TED talk given by Brene Brown. "Listening to Shame", https://www.ted.com/talks/brene_brown_listening_to_shame (March 2012, accessed November 29, 2023).

kid in my class. I don't recall many physical bully situations, but there were plenty of auditory ones, like mean kids calling me "fat boy" or "fatso." Hearing the words "fat boy" to this day hurts.

With the weight issues and all that hurt and rejection came loneliness. Oh, I had my friends and I loved hanging out with them, but I faced the ultimate adolescent rejection of not going on dates. I connected this to my heavy-set appearance. I'm not saying that I was right, but it was the story I told myself and that, therefore, limited me. I will describe that process in just a bit. It's the title of this chapter, after all!

Besides a disastrous blind double-date set up by my best friend, I didn't date in high school. I also didn't date in college. I met my wife in seminary and was shocked she wanted me to sit by her in class. We were like Beauty and the Beast.[5]

I also have had multiple sclerosis (MS) my entire adult life. I have been told by doctors that one side effect of the medication I take is depression, but I always felt that was redundant. Being physically weak and bodily numb were so depressing! In the earliest days of the disease, I was so weak. I recall one incident when I could barely stand at the urinal and one of my fraternity brothers stood by me and offered me the backside of his shoulder to lean on. I couldn't bring cans of soda to my mouth. Various parts and sections of my body would go numb for weeks at a time. Using a pencil felt like trying to play a piano with mittens on. The light-headedness and the balance issues were the worst. And these were my so-called "invincible" 20s!

MS maintained the depression I felt I already had. The bullying had influenced me in feeling rejected. In addition to rejection, I felt lonely. On top of all that, I felt both physically weak and numb. Many people began to pity me. But my depression story doesn't stop there. Now the losses came. At

---

5 Gary Trousdale, Kirk Wise, Alan Menken, Danny Troob and Michael Starobin. BEAUTY AND THE BEAST. USA, 1991.

the time of the writing of this chapter, my wife and I have said goodbye to three of our five children. Esther died in the delivery room after being born alive. Lily's pregnancy miscarried. Grace died towards the end of her pregnancy while her twin sister survived. Jen and I are so privileged to have Joshua and Julia as our precious children. But we also miss the babies we lost.

I have also experienced the sudden death of my father. I received a phone call on a Sunday morning informing me that Dad had complications and that he wouldn't be leaving the hospital. At the time I lived over three hours away and was unable to get downstate in time to say goodbye in person. I remember saying my last words to Dad over speakerphone as my downstate family gathered around his hospital bed one final time. This was before video chats were the huge thing that they are today. Dad was unconscious. But hey, they say people in that state are still able to listen, right? Life doesn't prepare you to compose final words as the gravity of your loved one's death suddenly hits you. I recall tearfully proclaiming the best words I could in such a moment.

I have had depressing situations and circumstances in my crawlspace for well over half of my life. Some of those are more recent and others go back quite a while. But depression is depression. Well-meaning individuals would often tell me that life would get better. Christian friends would remind me that God loves me. Those words were nice and came from a good place, but they didn't feel helpful. As a pastor, I would journey with people over the years who faced depression and I recall never really having much of an answer for them besides just listening to their pain and letting them know they weren't alone. It was frustrating, because I didn't have a specific answer for myself, either.

As part of my counselor training I read many helpful books. And one book made a key difference in my depression journey as a man, a pastor, and as a counselor—*Out of the Blues: Dealing with the Blues of Depression and Loneliness* by Wayne Mack (Focus Publishing, 2006). I highly recommend you buy yourself a copy. Reading his book, I struck depression gold.

Mack wrote, "We must learn to talk to ourselves rather than listening to ourselves…Talking to ourselves can prevent problems in the first place, but listening to ourselves almost always makes problems worse…When we talk to ourselves, we consciously direct our thoughts in a particular way."[6]
And I'll never forget that Mack tied this principle of talking to oneself to Psalm 42. Every new person I journey with who is depressed visits The Depression Psalm!

Why are you cast down, O my soul, and why are you in turmoil within me? Hope in God; for I shall again praise him, my salvation and my God. (Psalm 42:11)

The sons of Korah saw their situation like a sheep that had been cast down. In that situation, the sheep was helpless and hopeless on its back until the shepherd came along with his staff to set it back up. But rather than merely accepting their situation and marinating in their depression, the sons of Korah went to war with the one offensive weapon they had—their self-talk. That's right, they talked to themselves. Depression is maintained by self-talk. The story or narrative you maintain is what keeps you feeling depressed.

So they talked to their very soul. It might have sounded like this: "Why do you feel like that hopeless, downcast sheep? Put your hope in God. You'll praise him again! He's your salvation! The Shepherd is coming with his staff to put you back on your feet."

So this illustrates Mack's point perfectly. Rather than listening to yourself and letting that inform how you feel, talk to yourself and direct how you feel! The principle is that with your self-talk you influence your thoughts and those thoughts influence your feelings.

---

6 Mack, Wayne. *Out of the Blues: Dealing with the Blues of Depression & Loneliness.* (Focus Publishing, 2006). Bemidji, MN. pp. 72-73

What you consistently tell yourself either maintains or attacks your depression. Tell yourself good things about God. Replace your destructive self-talk with good truths from the Bible. Go to war daily using your self-talk. There is hope in the midst of depression!

I am not intending to reduce your depression journey to something simple or easy. I have found nothing easy in my years facing depression! But there is so much about my journey I simply can't control or maintain influence over. Going to war against my depressing thoughts has given me something helpful and powerful on which I can focus. Maybe this will be your first step in dealing with your depression. But let's make it a good one!

I realize that reading this is easier said than done. Earlier in the chapter, I mentioned depression's horrible partner, shame. I know in my experience with depression, I was tempted to repeat the stories about myself from my past. These stories were often judgmental in nature. I would find myself having done something bad and then the shame would craft the narrative that I *was* something bad. As a result of the bullying, I began to believe that my worth as a person was found in how others viewed me.

My children sometimes did this during the drama-filled toddler years. My wife and I would correct their behavior and they would respond by saying that they were the worst kid ever. Children might do this to manipulate a response out of their parents. I know we always responded by saying something like, "No, you are not the worst. You are not a bad kid. You made a bad choice." Shame creeps into our stories so easily as adults, though!

I recently accomplished the goal of losing 50 pounds. I couldn't wait to celebrate with social media pictures and posts. The fact that I would do so motivated me on my journey! And when people saw me were quick to congratulate and encourage. Deep within me, I recalled thinking two kinds of thoughts. The first one was to deflect from the good work that

I had done, because I felt like I had been overweight for far too long and thus didn't truly deserve the praise. The second one imagined what went through people's mind when they saw me. Sure I had lost 50 pounds, but I was still a very large man.

So conversationally I was gracious and thankful. I even shared the plan I had utilized to lose weight with those looking for pointers. But then I unearthed the shame statement, "This is a good start, but I know I have a long way to go." I was hoping for agreement as if I had staved off potential attack. I was used to people using my weight to value me, so it felt natural to not be too excited. To their credit, my friends gave me no indication that they viewed me that way or along those categories. I had no need to justify anything about my story. I had no need to get defensive or to deflect. My shame had produced within me a false reality that I was motivated to avoid.

Many years ago, when I was dating the woman who would later become my wife, I recalled her getting upset at my sarcastic, self-deprecating humor. I would make jokes about my own weight and she didn't like it. She told me that she didn't view me that way. She was quick to respond that she was enjoying dating me and journeying alongside me. I remember thinking that a gorgeous woman like her had no business dating an overweight person like me. We would walk on dates together holding hands. I swore I saw people judging me as we passed them. Every time I felt like I had to justify my existence in her life, I would remember her words. It would be the first of many times when she would disarm my shame narrative. One of the greatest things my wife has ever done is to remind me that not only does she love me, but so does God.

Where I see shame show up in other people, it usually involves things centered around value. They felt lacking or unworthy in some manner. I ask them two basic questions. First, what do they use to determine their value? I ask them to consider what they have accomplished (or haven't accomplished). Usually the ones struggling with unemployment or purpose begin to reveal their shame here.

Next, I lead them to consider what life-state they are in. Here is where the lonely, the unmarried, and the childless have something to say. Maybe the person compares and contrasts themself with their community. This is similar to the previous question, but it brings other people into the story. So if other friends were married or had jobs or were having children, this would affect their story here.

Finally in this opening question, I ask if they are faithful to a standard they set for themselves. Shame statements tied to value would bring up the fact that they felt like a horrible parent because other people's children were more well-behaved. Or they saw their career development as lacking when contrasted to their peers in the same field. Self-judgment thrives on such standards.

So let's take a moment to unearth foundations for your stories. Is your value tied to a *what?* Please list some items under each category.

What things have you accomplished?

What life-state are you in?

How do you compare or contrast with your community?

How are you faithful to the standard you set for yourself?

It is at this point that I reveal my biblical strategy. A *what* has no business determining your value. The things about your life are unable to determine your worth. A person's worth is inherent and foundational to their identity.[7] It is not able to be increased or decreased by the events and accomplishments of life.

So at this point I leave the *what* category and transition to the *who.* I ask how others have sought to determine their value. Here is where those who have been bullied quietly speak up. I hear also from the abandoned and the divorced. Or the ones who never lived up to someone else's expectations of them. <u>Many of the stories we tell ourselves are simply repeated messages from other people trying to devalue us.</u>

At this point, I ask how they value themselves. It's been my experience that between measuring life experiences and the input from other people, a person already has their value story lined up. When they talk about their situations, they slip in words of judgment. The shame speaks clearly in moments like those.

---

7 For further exploration of this theological truth, I highly recommend the masterful book *Created in God's Image* by Anthony A. Hoekema (William B. Eerdmans Publishing Company, 1994). Grand Rapids, MI.

How have others tried to determine your value?

How have you tried to determine your value?

I try to bring comfort by reminding them that not only can a *what* not determine their value, but also neither can a *who.* Value statements can be spoken by ourselves or others, but that doesn't mean they describe reality. <u>Just because they feel worthless doesn't mean that they are.</u>

Things cannot determine your inherent value. Neither can others or even oneself. The only other character that remains in a person's story is God. Does God have the capacity to proclaim the inherent worth of a person? My argument is that He can and He does.

For you formed my inward parts you knitted me together in my mother's womb. I praise you, for I am fearfully and wonderfully made. Wonderful are your works; my soul knows it very well. (Psalm 139:13-14)

This psalm proclaims the value of mankind. Each person is a wonderful work of God. As image bearers of God (Genesis 1:26-27) we are inherently worthy of respect and honor. God thus proclaims our value according to His will and His standard. We have that value even before we are born. But it doesn't stop there. Read how much God values you!

...but God shows his love for us in that while we were still sinners, Christ died for us. (Romans 5:8)

Blessed be the God and Father of our Lord Jesus Christ, who has blessed us in Christ with every spiritual blessing in the heavenly places, even as he chose us in him before the foundation of the world, that we should be holy and blameless before him. In love he predestined us for adoption to himself as sons through Jesus Christ, according to the purpose of his will, to the praise of his glorious grace, with which he has blessed us. In him we have redemption through his blood, the forgiveness of our trespasses, according to the riches of his grace, which he lavished on us... (Ephesians 1:3-8)

These two passages are not only convicting, but also encouraging. How much are you valued by God? Dear Christian, he sent Christ to die for you. He chose you, predestined you, loved you, has given you grace, redeemed you, forgiven you, and lavished rich blessings upon you! I would say that God values you. <u>The very God who can proclaim your value, does.</u>

So now these verses have filled your quiver with beautiful self-talk arrows to fire. Let's redirect those thoughts. Here are a few examples. *I feel fat and worthless.* No, I am wonderfully made! *Nobody loves me.* No, I am loved by God! *My life has no meaning.* No, Christ died for me. Look how important God considers me!

The stories you tell yourself involve other people, yourself, and God. Let's take a moment and consider those stories. You may not be journeying with depression and shame, but you most likely maintain pivotal internal stories. Like we did in chapter 1 with what you want, here let's record the big stories of your life.

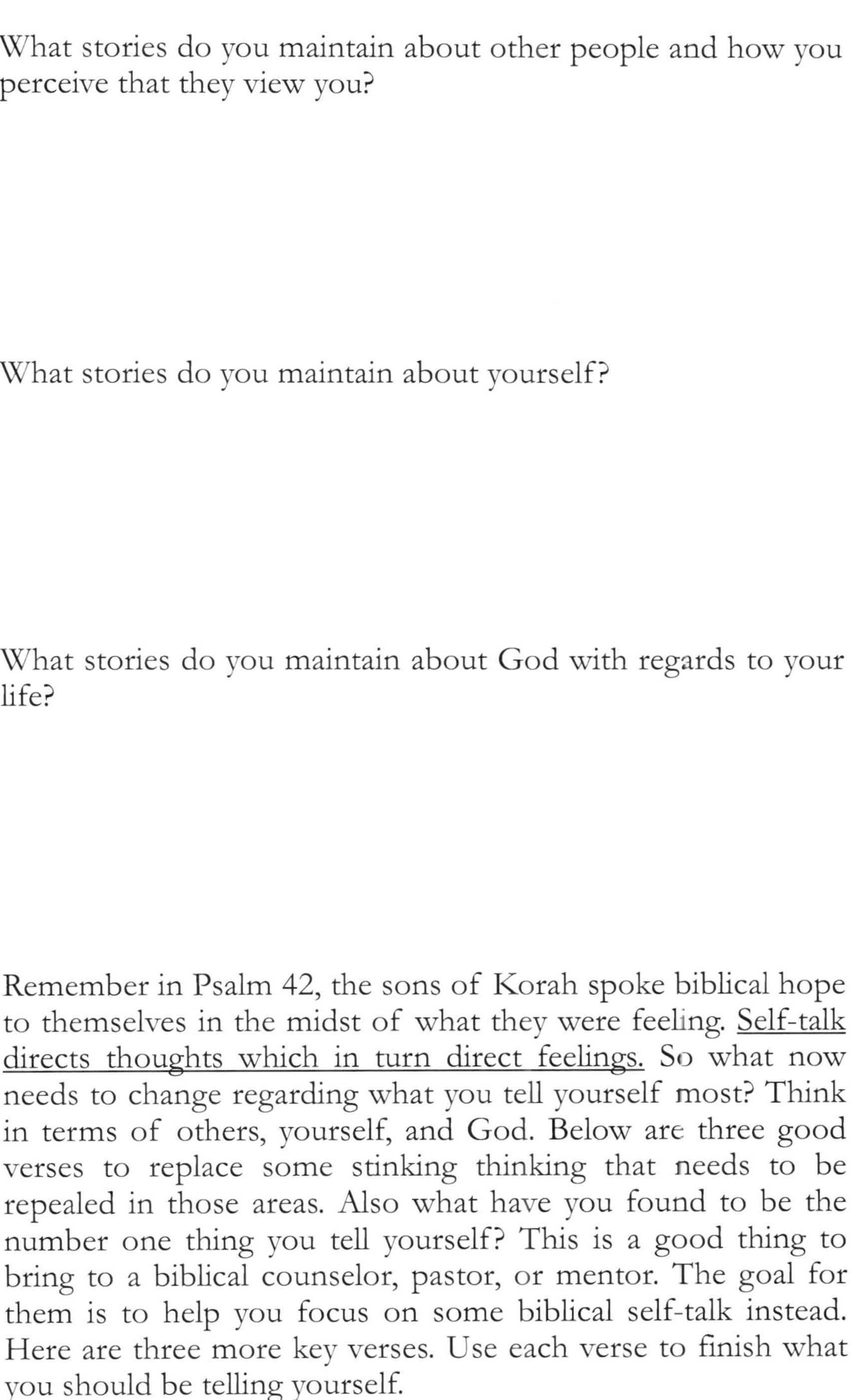

What stories do you maintain about other people and how you perceive that they view you?

What stories do you maintain about yourself?

What stories do you maintain about God with regards to your life?

Remember in Psalm 42, the sons of Korah spoke biblical hope to themselves in the midst of what they were feeling. Self-talk directs thoughts which in turn direct feelings. So what now needs to change regarding what you tell yourself most? Think in terms of others, yourself, and God. Below are three good verses to replace some stinking thinking that needs to be repealed in those areas. Also what have you found to be the number one thing you tell yourself? This is a good thing to bring to a biblical counselor, pastor, or mentor. The goal for them is to help you focus on some biblical self-talk instead. Here are three more key verses. Use each verse to finish what you should be telling yourself.

But I say to you, love your enemies and pray for those who persecute you. (Matthew 5:44)

Based upon this verse, regarding others I need to focus my thought on…

The LORD is my shepherd, I shall not want. (Psalm 23:1)

Based upon this verse, God does what for me…

And [Jesus] said to his disciples, "Therefore I tell you, do not be anxious about your life, what you will eat, nor about your body, what you will put on. For life is more than food, and the body more than clothing. Consider the ravens: they neither sow nor reap, they have neither storehouses nor barn, and yet God feeds them. Of how much more value are you than the birds! (Luke 12:22-24)

Based upon this passage, I need to tell myself…

I hope your crawlspace is getting clearer. Thank you for doing the hard work of considering these questions regarding your heart. I next want to tackle an issue that affects so many: anxiety. In fact, you might have just read that passage from Luke 12 right above and panicked a bit. Anxiety is real for so many and my prayer is that answering our next question will provide further direction and hope.

CHAPTER 3

WHAT CAN YOU CONTROL?

"Oh my goodness, is everyone OK?" I asked this question immediately to my family.

"I'm sorry." I said this one to my wife.

Looking to the left, I saw the bed of the semi-truck mere inches away. A terrifying moment had just come to an end and the anxiety was just beginning.

I had been driving the family car in a lane approaching a tollbooth that wasn't open so I decided to change lanes to one that was. The problem was that for the first time in as long as I can remember, I refused to do the over-the-shoulder lane check. Thus, I missed the large truck in my blindspot. I consider myself a good driver, but I was not one that day.

Our small car had collided with the truck in a perfectly horizontal fashion. Thus damage was done to the side of our vehicle, but nothing penetrated into the cabin. As the truck had braked, its inertia still had carried our car into the concrete wall of the tollbooth lane. Our car's exterior frame had been damaged to the point that our trip to Grandma's came to a screeching halt, literally.

What would you do in such a moment? I received affirmatives to my first question from my wife and kids. Regarding my second statement, I jokingly think an angel supernaturally closed my wife's mouth. Throughout the whole ordeal she remained supportive and helpful rather than criticizing me and shaming me. I will never forget her supportive attitude during that time and in the weeks to come.

I immediately took stock of our situation. The kids were safe in the backseat. My wife had some soreness from where the seatbelt crossed her shoulder. My glasses had flown off my face and my coffee cup in the console had delivered its contents all over the car. We were lodged into the side of the truck's trailer. I couldn't even open my door to exchange insurance information with the other driver. So, the day after Thanksgiving we were stuck on an interstate highway outside Chicago.

As I sat there with my thoughts, Counselor Joel came to mind. What do I counsel in such moments? When the people I journey with express anxiety in their situations, I invite them to ask two questions. I call them the "control" questions. What about your situation **can you not** control? What about your situation **can** you control?

So I pondered the first question. There was so much I couldn't control. I couldn't control what I had done. I couldn't control if my family was physically hurt or mentally frazzled. I couldn't even get my car unstuck from the side of the semi. The responses of everyone else were outside of my control, as well. The other driver, my wife, my kids, the policeman, the insurance agents, the cab driver, the tow truck, my downstate family…I had no control over these things.

Many people face situations like this with so many things they can't control and they get stuck. This is because they focus on those things where they are inherently powerless. To invest here is to make the anxiety worse. It's to feed it unnecessarily.

It's been my experience regarding mental health struggles that depression is something that is maintained, but anxiety is something that is fed. The main culprits that feed anxiety are fear, worry, anger, and jealousy. If you are a control-freak reading this, anxieties flow from your inability to manage the things you wish you could.

I remember praying out loud to God with thanksgiving and gratefulness. The truck was inches away from killing me, but also the same distance from killing my five-year-old daughter in the seat directly behind me. This realization still haunts me in occasional quiet moments. I still thank God for keeping my family safe that day.

So what could I control? By God's grace, the car still was running, so we had heat. The phones still could be charged. Thus, we started making our phone calls. We called 911 and got a police officer to come to the wreckage. He arranged for a highway tow truck to assist us. The police officer handled the communication between me and the other driver. I was issued a citation and he gave us instructions on what we were to do next.

The tow truck driver had to literally drag us perpendicularly from the semi. I couldn't see any damage to the large truck as he did so. We remember him getting back on the road in a reasonably quick manner. We were directed to pass through the toll and then park our car in the shoulder past the tollbooth. And so with tires blown our vehicle made a *hunka-chunka-hunka-chunka* sound as we got the car positioned over there.

We were informed that we could leave the car on the side of the interstate for a couple of hours, but that we had to arrange transportation away from that spot. So Jennifer and I got to work manning the phones. We called downstate informing my extended family about our situation. They generously offered to come get us, but we were hours away from them, closer to our home than theirs. We called our insurance agent and began to arrange for both a tow truck and a taxi. We had no address or intersection as we were on the interstate highway. Many taxi services have a policy to not pick up people from those locations, so we were at the mercy of what we could find. More things we couldn't control!

Jen and I could control our attitudes during that stressful time. She would make calls to family while I stayed on the phone with the insurance agent. Meanwhile, we were in this smashed car running on the side of the highway with cars zooming by. Eventually we were able to arrange both a taxi for us (and our luggage!) and a tow truck for our car. Thankfully the insurance agent arranged for a repair shop close to our house to receive the towed car. We were about an hour away from home and well over two hours away from my extended family downstate. Our Thanksgiving trip ended with us returning home with one car missing from the driveway.

Jen and I had focused on our attitudes. We both remained outwardly calm during the whole ordeal. Jen wasn't sniping at me for being careless and therefore wasn't agreeing with the shame story I was already telling myself in my thoughts. That story was that I had ruined everything. I needed to do the work of our previous chapter regarding stories and depression! We intentionally maintained control over our emotions and were good examples for our children. We sent back a phone to the backseat so they could watch a cartoon to pass the time. Travel snacks were eaten while we waited. The control questions had gotten me through an afternoon of high anxiety. I had focused on what I could control and hadn't dwelt on what I couldn't. I had also gotten a new illustration to use with counselees!

I've journeyed with people who have had fears and worries that kept them up at night. Some have endured relationships that felt messy or broken and they dreaded facing the other person. Anxiety can be centered in our political and social issues. It also can dwell on spiritual and apocalyptic fears. I've had friends with anxiety concerning governmental systems and others regarding the demonic. Finances can bring worry. Medical diagnoses can carry panic. The future never seems to officially arrive, but it sure loves to feed anxiety! What can you control and what can you not control?

I remember our first pregnancy. My wife and I had a difficult experience when we had that first ultrasound. We remember the technician making strange murmurs and stopping the taking of baby measurements. They staff had ushered us into a special room and asked us to wait. We were eventually told that the doctor would see us. After some time we were told that they couldn't locate a heartbeat for the baby. The doctor told us that we would need to schedule another appointment to perform a follow-up procedure that he deemed necessary.

We left the doctor's office that day both shocked and worried. We had previously made plans to share the good news about the baby to family and friends. Yet, we entered the weekend with heavy hearts. I remember that Saturday night well, for we had hosted an outreach event at our church. I recall a friend who came up to me and asked how I was doing. After explaining how that day had gone, I told him that we were both sad and afraid. Our situation had us worried. Even though this was years ago, I'll never forget the next moment. My friend looked at me concerned and with a critical tone to his voice said, "The Bible tells us not to be anxious. I can't believe you are worried. You are a pastor. Shame on you."

Did my friend have a point? The passage he was referencing is in Philippians 4.

…do not be anxious about anything, but in everything by prayer and supplication with thanksgiving let your requests be made known to God. And the peace of God, which surpasses all understanding, will guard your hearts and your minds in Christ Jesus. (Philippians 4:6-7)

Some people read that passage and are definitely not a fan. I've even had people tell me that the Bible is not relatable here. Some of you reading these verses might even feel the same way about them as you do about my friend and what he said to me years ago!

I'm very thankful that the man God inspired to write these words knew what anxiety was. Paul was clear in his writings that he journeyed with anxiety. He described a daily anxiety for the churches he planted (2 Corinthians 11:28). He spoke of opponents who had the power to cause him anxiety or "add to his chains" during his imprisonment (Philippians 1:17).

Thus, the Philippians 4 command has the flavor of the "sin" argument in 1 John 2:1-2. Are you familiar with those verses?

My little children, I am writing these things to you so that you may not sin. But if anyone does sin, we have an advocate with the Father, Jesus Christ the righteous. He is the propitiation for our sins, and not for ours only but also for the sins of the whole world. (1 John 2:1-2)

John wrote in verse one that his audience may not sin, but then in verse two described Jesus as the advocate for the sinner. A goal of the Christian life is not to sin, but if and when you do, you have an advocate in Christ Jesus.

So do we see that tension with what the Bible says regarding anxiety? We in fact do. Peter once wrote one of the most comforting verses in the Bible regarding anxiety.

Humble yourselves, therefore, under the mighty hand of God so that at the proper time he may exalt you, casting all your anxieties on him, because he cares for you. (1 Peter 5:6-7)

So live with that tension the same way as with what John said above about sin. Don't be anxious, but when you do have anxiety, cast it upon God. Rather than living in shame for having anxiety, take that anxiety and give it to God. You have an answer when you are anxious. And that answer is to go to God with it.

This is actually how Paul "landed the plane" with the Philippians. My control questions flow from his argument. **The things you can't control are therefore moments to trust God.** Paul commanded them in those moments to pray to God and make their requests known with an attitude of thanksgiving. Could you imagine if, in the midst of your anxiety, you stopped and thanked God for an opportunity to trust him?

The moments you can control are opportunities to honor and obey God. This comes from Paul's next set of verses.

Finally, brothers, whatever is true, whatever is honorable, whatever is just, whatever is pure, whatever is lovely, whatever is commendable, if there is any excellence, if there is anything worthy of praise, think about these things. What you have learned and received and heard and seen in me—practice these things, and the God of peace will be with you. (Philippians 4:8-9)

The inside you is governed by what you think, and the outside you is reflected in what you practice. In those verses, Paul summarized the whole person who honors God. In verses 7 and 9, Paul gave promises. The first was the peace of God guarding your heart and mind. The second was Immanuel—the God of peace will be with you. <u>So in the midst of your anxiety, the peace you crave most is promised if you respond God's way.</u> You get His peace with you and even God Himself with you!

A few months ago, my family needed that peace. We had just adopted two older dogs from a rescue agency. Over the course of the rest of the weekend, the dogs never left my wife's side. So we were unprepared for the shock of Monday morning.

When Jen exited the house, both dogs bolted right past her and outside the door. They were like Jen's shadow all weekend, so we thought nothing of either of them running into the yard. In fact, Jen was able to call the Chihuahua right back to her. But the Bichon not only ignored both of our calls, but ran directly towards the busiest street in our area. I chased after her calling her name again and again, but I quickly found out that her four legs were clearly faster than my two!

It was an all-hands-on-deck kind of moment. Jen had to go to work, but I was home on my day off with the kids. So I quickly got our children into the car and we slowly started driving in the direction the dog had run. "Kids, I will focus on driving. Will you start looking in the yards that we pass?"

Thinking our new dog would have been scared away from the busy road, I kept driving down various neighborhood streets. We simply couldn't find her. I remember Joshua and Julia saying they were scared, but then they decided to pray to God for help in finding her. "God, please help us find [Betty] and please take care of her until we do." Later that afternoon, God indeed answered both of those prayers.

I had been asking my control questions all morning. I couldn't control where our dog had run to or if she was safe. So I trusted God with those matters. There were some things that I could indeed control. Like with that auto wreck, I could control the attitude I had with my kids and with my wife. It was as if God kept my mouth supernaturally shut regarding her this time! She had felt horrible for letting the dogs get out the door. I kept calm and prayed alongside my kids. At the recommendation of friends, I also seized the opportunity to post information on various lost dog social media pages.

Later that afternoon, we decided to take our Chihuahua for a walk. A family member who has two dogs had thought that maybe our Bichon would respond if she was hiding nearby. We were running out of options of things to try. All of a sudden my phone rang. It was the adoption agency. Evidently Betty the Bichon had run over a mile down the busy road and entered into the yard of an older woman. The woman had gotten her inside and cleaned the street dust off her and then called her adult son. The son had then taken Betty to a local veterinarian who had read her identity microchip. I was planning on changing the identity and contact information on those chips during that week, but this had all happened before then! The chip still had Betty's previous Wisconsin address.

So when the agency up in Wisconsin called my phone and asked me if Betty had gotten lost I couldn't control what type of dog owner they thought I was. I, however, could control how I responded and in owning what I could own about our situation. I simply told the truth. They proceeded to tell me about Betty's grand adventure (reread it above if you would like) and then informed me she was en route to our address. Twenty minutes later, we had our lost dog back home. God had again provided for us in the midst of our anxiety. God literally had answered both aspects of my children's prayers. My wife was overjoyed when I started texting her pictures. She called me with excited tears at her first opportunity.

It was another moment to trust God with what I couldn't control and honor Him with what I could. How about your life? Let's take a moment and work through your anxious situations.

What are you going through that is causing you worry, fear, stress, or anxiety?

What about your situations can you NOT control?

What would it look like to trust God with those?

What about your situations CAN you control?

What would it look like to honor and obey God with those?

Looking back at my stories, I marvel at the care and provision of God. But I don't want you to think that I have always responded perfectly to the anxieties of life. I have countless other examples where I trusted God but didn't honor God. Or others where I responded in a manner that communicated I didn't really trust God. Many times in my past I have responded to anxiety with worry and impatience. I remember at least one season when I distracted myself with sinful attitudes or unhealthy habits. <u>I don't have many victories in this area. But the control questions work</u>. They have enabled me to direct my thoughts on God and not on myself. After the Thanksgiving car wreck and the "Betty the Bolter" incident, I was left simply marveling at God's faithfulness. I was and am thankful for God's shepherding of my responses.

Chapter One helped us to understand our primary desires and motivations. Chapter Two focused on the stories that we tell ourselves. This chapter introduced you to the control questions. As we continue to explore the crawlspace of the heart, our next chapter ponders the very matters that show up in our responses and attitudes. You're going to take a look at your "branches."

CHAPTER 4

WHAT IS ON YOUR BRANCHES?

Many years ago, I worked at a major department store unloading the delivery trucks. At the start of each shift, the managers sent our crew to a special room at the back of the store which contained a large conveyer belt. Each one of us received a booth alongside the belt and was given a number. As items emerged from the truck and down the conveyer into our room, we would each look for our number and start making stacks of our boxes as they passed by. After the truck was unloaded, we then would be given a section of the store to re-stock empty spaces on the shelves with the items in the boxes.

Occasionally I would be given the toy section and would empty the boxes of toys and put them on the shelves in the right spots. I'll never forget one time when some toy collectors followed me around as I opened boxes. These particular men were collectors of little metal toy cars. I recall one collector who offered to open the boxes for me and to stock the shelves himself if only I would first let him dig through the toys in the box! Sadly, they had to painfully wait for me to actually put each item on the shelf.

One of the questions I remembered asking during one cold Wisconsin morning as we waited for our boxes beside that conveyer belt was how the store knew what to order for the next truck? I was told that there was a central computerized system that oversaw things. Whenever a customer purchased an item, the barcode which was scanned triggered the computer to order a replacement for that item. Each new box that I took off the conveyer belt was directly related to a previous purchase. So each one of those toy collectors who purchased a little metal car caused the system to replace that item with another. And from my understanding, the toys in that series would come from a randomized collection, so they never knew which ones in the series would arrive. This must of been why they were so interested in my boxes!

I remember being fascinated by that system. It was a wonderful way to keep stock of their shelves. The system knew exactly how many of an item the store had and when they would be receiving new ones. I almost wanted to go and purchase an obscure item from a less popular aisle of the store just to see if the next truck delivered a replacement! Yet, I recall being on too tight a budget during that season of life for such a thing.

I think of that cold conveyer belt from time to time. It represented a store that knew exactly what stock it had to sell. I have journeyed with men and women who wished they were closer to God. They would tell me that God felt distant to them. They wished things were different and thus had come to me or were sent my way for help. They would confess things in their lives that shouldn't be there and things they wished instead were there. Over and over again that department store and its fancy computerized system came to mind. I began to ponder if only there was a way for the Christian to take stock of their spiritual shelves? We could then ponder what's present and also what's missing. Does the Bible give us a system that helps us in this area much like that computer helped the store?

My point in this chapter is that the Bible indeed does help us answer that question. I invite you to the 15th chapter of the

Gospel of John. In Chapter 14, Jesus not only gave us the majestic verse six (look it up if you don't have it memorized!), but also promised the Helper, the Holy Spirit, whom the Father would send in Jesus' name. Jesus promised that the Holy Spirit would remind the believer of the teachings of Jesus (14:26). Chapter 16 continued with the promise of the Spirit guiding believers into all the truth from Jesus (16:13-14). So we get the idea from Jesus that the believer grows because of the work of the Holy Spirit. So let us read the famous section in Chapter 15.

"I am the true vine, and my Father is the vinedresser. Every branch in me that does not bear fruit he takes away, and every branch that does bear fruit he prunes, that it may bear more fruit. Already you are clean because of the word that I have spoken to you. Abide in me, and I in you. As the branch cannot bear fruit by itself, unless it abides in the vine, neither can you, unless you abide in me. I am the vine; you are the branches.

Whoever abides in me and I in him, he it is that bears much fruit, for apart from me you can do nothing. If anyone does not abide in me he is thrown away like a branch and withers; and the branches are gathered, thrown into the fire, and burned. If you abide in me, and my words abide in you, ask whatever you wish, and it will be done for you. By this my Father is glorified, that you bear much fruit and so prove to be my disciples. (John 15:1-8)

Sounds like a great place to start. These words of Jesus should hit home in your heart. Reading them causes a person to consider a number of questions. Am I bearing fruit like I should? Is the Father pruning me or not? Am I truly abiding in Jesus? Am I indeed proving to be Jesus' disciple and giving glory to the Father? Every one of those questions is like stepping on a weight scale after a long time of not doing so.

Every time I've done so, one part of me was terrified of the answer and the other part of me was relieved to have gotten the results so I could start focusing on the right things all over again!

We learn from these verses that bearing fruit is a matter of God's sovereign work in us. A person only grows fruit as they abide in Jesus. To abide is to continue, to stay, and to remain. After a big storm I always find tree branches lying in my yard. Those branches always wither and die. Their leaves brown and crumble. This is because they no longer abide in the tree. Since I don't build many fires, I simply collect the branches and put them in a special garbage can for pickup day. They have no other use to me.

This passage reminds us to abide in Jesus. The way we do so is when His words abide in us. This is why these verses are between both of the "Holy Spirit themed" speeches in Chapters 14 and 16. We need the Holy Spirit to help the words of Jesus to remain in us. We require His guidance and shepherding on a daily basis. Thus whatever fruit that is grown in our lives is under the sovereign plan of the Father, remaining in the Son, and directed by the Spirit.

We therefore have a Trinity moment here. God the Son spoke of God the Father being glorified if believers like you and me bear fruit on our branches. God the Holy Spirit is the one who oversees this process much like that computer from my story oversaw the stock of the department store. Since the Father, the Son, and the Holy Spirit are involved in this process, we must ask a question of great importance. This is the fourth question on the journey to explore the crawlspace of the heart.

What fruit is on the branches of the tree of your life?

Let's now ponder a very famous passage in the New Testament. I have used these verses to illustrate our question. We are grateful for Paul's letter to the Galatians for it assists us with the expectations of Jesus. Galatians 5 describes John 15.

But I say, walk by the Spirit, and you will not gratify the desires of the flesh. For the desires of the flesh are against the Spirit, and the desires of the Spirit are against the flesh, for these are opposed to each other, to keep you from doing the things you want to do. But if you are led by the Spirit, you are not under the law. Now the works of the flesh are evident: sexual immorality, impurity, sensuality, idolatry, sorcery, enmity, strife, jealousy, fits of anger, rivalries, dissensions, divisions, envy, drunkenness, orgies, and things like these. I warn you, as I warned you before, that those who do such things will not inherit the kingdom of God.

But the fruit of the Spirit is love, joy, peace, patience, kindness, goodness, faithfulness, gentleness, self-control; against such things there is no law. And those who belong to Christ Jesus have crucified the flesh with its passions and desires. If we live by the Spirit, let us also keep in step with the Spirit. Let us not become conceited, provoking one another, envying one another. (Galatians 5:16-26)

So let's take a moment and walk through this passage. It starts with an either/or. <u>You are either being led by the Holy Spirit or by yourself.</u> This was a drum that Paul continued to beat as he addressed the church at Galatia. A person is justified by faith and not by works (2:16). So you are either depending upon that which is from the Spirit or the works from your own flesh to save you. The curse of the law is tied to our efforts (3:10).

Our flesh can never do enough on its own to please God or to result in our being justified. We need faith, which is trusting God over ourselves. The flesh is therefore a horrible leader for the Christian. So our passage first asks who is leading you? It's either the Spirit or your desires. And they are enemies. This is why Jesus said that his followers begin by denying themselves, not following themselves (Luke 9:23).

Next, there are two lists of fruit. Have you ever been at a conference and the host approaches the podium and says that the person he is introducing needs no introduction? That would be this first list. You and I have advanced graduate "degrees" in sin. We are by nature masters of this list. The fruits of the flesh describe issues both within an individual and in relationships. We feel convicted reading this first list of fruits. If you currently feel distant from God, I would invite you to ask who or what is leading the way you live your life. If you are being led by your fleshly desires, the fruit your life displays will reflect that. If you are led by the Holy Spirit, you will be producing different fruit. One of the reasons the department store computer worked so well was that it responded to the direct data fed into the system. The fruit you display is a direct result of the leader you follow in life. You either are led by the Spirit or by your own fleshly desires.

Remember a few paragraphs ago when I mentioned the sovereignty of the Holy Spirit regarding growing fruits on your branches? The second list describes those fruits. If you grew up in church you no doubt heard of them referred to as the Fruits of the Spirit. The fruit on your branches is either produced by the flesh or by the Spirit. And if by the Spirit they are His fruits that He sovereignly grows in and through you.

Let's ask some questions that will help you take stock of the fruit present on your branches. First, let's remind ourselves from Galatians 5 of the fruit we don't or shouldn't want there.

Now the works of the flesh are evident: sexual immorality, impurity, sensuality, idolatry, sorcery, enmity, strife, jealousy, fits of anger, rivalries, dissensions, divisions, envy, drunkenness, orgies, and things like these. (19-21a)

Those verses provide us with a great moment for introspection! Picture your life as a tree with branches. And for just a moment those branches are empty, but you know they really are not. On those empty branches start to draw or write fruits that you see. Are there any fruits present from this first list? You know how this works by now. Time to own your situation and write these fruits down.

What fruit is on your branches from this list that shouldn't be there?

Thank you for writing them down. You might feel guilt and shame reading your list. I would counsel you to listen to what you are feeling. Whenever I write my list God works on me. I feel ashamed and upset at myself. To ignore those feelings is to miss the point. Now, I don't recommend wallowing in that shame or hating yourself, but let that conviction you are feeling do its work. A major reason you are feeling distant from God is that you have been cherishing sins in your heart.

You might rationalize your list or have excuses at the ready. You possibly defend yourself or get defensive regarding the position you are in and those fruits that you see on your list. <u>Your only hope is to repent.</u> I want you to picture your life, your marriage, your parenting, your friendships, your workplace, and your social media next. We'll describe repentance more in a moment. For now, just dream a bit.

What would change about you if you stopped growing those fruits on your branches?

What is at risk if you don't take this fruit exercise seriously and don't desire change?

Now, let's move towards the second set of fruit. You want, or should want, to see these on your branches. Let's read those verses again from Galatians 5.

But the fruit of the Spirit is love, joy, peace, patience, kindness, goodness, faithfulness, gentleness, self-control; against such things there is no law. (22-23)

What fruit is not present from this list that should be on your branches?

This introspection can also hurt. You might feel regret or even jealousy here. You might even find yourself feeling angry with God for just a moment or finding that you are resentful or bitter because you don't have a fruit that others seem to have. You might possibly even continue to justify or make excuses for your branches based upon the life situations that you have endured. Your only hope here is to pray. <u>Ask God to sovereignly grow that fruit on your branches.</u> Just know that as He does so, He may put you in situations where you need to show that fruit.

What situation does God have you in today that would grow that fruit in your life? How is God leading and convicting you right now?

Contemplate for a moment the wife who struggled with her frustrated emotional reactions toward her husband. She no doubt listed *anger* from that first list. She also recognized that if she didn't repent, her marriage was never going to improve. On her second list, she noticed that *patience* wasn't there but should be. So she began to pray to God for patience. Over time she even came to realize that her husband provided a perfect illustration for her heart issue. She was challenged to see the sovereign hand of God as He used her difficult husband to spur growth in her. When she felt most angry and impatient she prayed for God to change her and to sovereignly work in her to grow the patience she needed.

Or consider the young man addicted to pornography. *Sexual immorality* was on his first list. He realized that if he didn't repent that not only would his hypocrisy continue, but he would one day bring that into his future marriage. The big omission from the second fruit list was *self-control*. So he prayed for God to grow that fruit on his branches. He trusted God in those moments when he wanted to do otherwise. He got help and sought accountability with other men who would pray for him and challenge him. He was intentional and God grew that fruit on his branches.

<u>To confess is to agree with God about the nature of your two lists.</u> "God, I agree with Galatians 5 that what I see on my branches from the first list is a problem. Unless I change, nothing will change."

There it is. That is what I needed during my younger years. I certainly confessed my sins to God, and I probably gave nominal claims to have repented. But did my branches reveal that I had been keeping with that repentance? Absolutely not. If they had they would have shown a fruit of the Spirit rather than a fruit of the flesh. To truly repent is to keep with the Spirit. It all goes back to Galatians 5 again. To keep with repentance is to remain in Jesus, the vine. It thus goes back to John 15, as well.

During the writing of this chapter I was asked to be a substitute Bible teacher for the Thursday ladies' small group at my church. I take a regular turn on Thursdays singing hymns with these ladies and playing my guitar. These women are some of my favorite people in the church and every time I see one of them at a weekend service it thrills me to greet them and their families. Since they gave me no direction as to what to teach that day, I decided to come with our question about the fruit on the branches. I gave them the same story you read concerning that department store and we worked through the same passages of Scripture. I even had printed out pictures of trees with bare branches for them to add the fruit they each noticed as they reflected.

But as I closed my time with them I noticed something strange. The ladies looked concerned at their tree worksheets. Some of them looked sad and others appeared angry or emotional. Some were just slowly shaking their heads. I've seen those kinds of looks before. They exist when people begin to ponder how life has turned out. They are looks of wonder and regret. My dear friend Terry used to love to quote me that famous line from the 1856 poem by John Greenleaf Whittier, "For all sad words of tongue and pen, the saddest are these, 'It might have been.'"[8]

So I asked the ladies to all look up at me. I shared with them that I was so proud of them for asking those difficult questions about their lives. I reassured them that I didn't see

---

8 Whittier, John Greenleaf. "Maud Muller" (1856)

their trees as withered and lifeless or devoid of fruit. I smiled and said that they are some of the greatest treasures of our church. Their trees stand as majestic as any redwood and full of fruit like in an orchard at harvest time. The lives they have lived are examples for all of us younger than them.

God had blessed their years with experience and wisdom. Their branches proudly displayed the fruit of decades of following Jesus. I then gently reminded them that even though my questions may have caused them to indeed desire to repent and to pray, that they were to do so with joy in their hearts. Even if they felt like their years on the vine were growing shorter, God was still pruning them for His glory. I noticed by that point that many of the frowns had begun to turn to smiles. The shaking of heads had transformed into nodding. I smiled with them and told the Thursday ladies that I would share this story in my book.

My talk that day was both challenging and encouraging to those ladies. I pray that this chapter did the same for you. In fact, I urge you to revisit this chapter again during a later season in your life. For you may at times feel distant from God and need to ask the tough questions to take stock all over again. It would be very convicting to read your previous answers. Had repentance really happened if you still struggle the same way you once did? Also revisiting those lists would be encouraging as you would see God's sovereignty at work in your life. There's space below if you would like to draw a tree and bravely place fruit there!

If your branches reveal the presence of selfish fruit, <u>it's time to repent</u>. If your branches reveal the absence of the Spirit's fruit, <u>it's time to pray</u>. What this all comes down to is intentionality. The areas in which you are most intentional are where you will see the change you need. To truly change requires intentionality and consistency. It's the question we will consider in the next chapter.

CHAPTER 5

WHERE ARE YOU INTENTIONAL?

"50 pounds. By the next Man Camp, I will lose 50 pounds."

Picture 200 men gathered in the great room of the Long House at a camp in rural Wisconsin.[9] Represented around the room were guys from multiple churches and cities. They were people of different ethnicities and backgrounds. Men who had bonded as brothers over an amazing, intentional weekend. At the end of the final day microphones had been placed for individuals to stand before the room and proclaim how they had been challenged or encouraged. I recall hearing men committing to be better husbands and fathers. Some who had felt convicted because of an addiction. Others proclaiming they would live differently. And I got up there and uttered that line. "By the next Man Camp, I will lose 50 pounds."

As I awaited my turn to stand behind the microphone, I kept thinking to myself *Do I actually want to do this? Once I say this I won't be able to walk it back. The guys will remember. This is going to be seen as my thing. But I need this. I can use this to fight my excuses. Oh*

9 "Man Camp" at The Woods Camp in Fredonia, WI. https://www.thewoodscamp.org/man-camp

God, may this be the moment I need.

I remember the room erupting in cheers. I can still picture the smiles. As I made my way back to my chair, I received hugs, high fives, fist bumps, and back slaps. I heard shouts of "Yeah, buddy!" and "Let's go!" It was a moment I would hold onto daily in the weeks and months to come. It was an intentional moment in my life.

<u>Intentionality defines how you have addressed the questions in this book.</u> What do you want most? You are most intentional to achieve that which you want. What stories do you maintain within yourself? That maintenance requires intentionality. What can you control? The things you can control are where you should be most intentional. What fruit is on your branches? These are the fruits that result from your intentional submission to God and remaining in His vine.

So let's take a moment and contemplate that intentionality. King David once prayed this prayer. Let's pause and have the Scripture do it's work.

Search me, O God, and know my heart! Try me and know my thoughts! And see if there be any grievous way in me, and lead me in the way everlasting! (Psalm 139:23-24)

What do your thoughts and feelings communicate to God or about God?

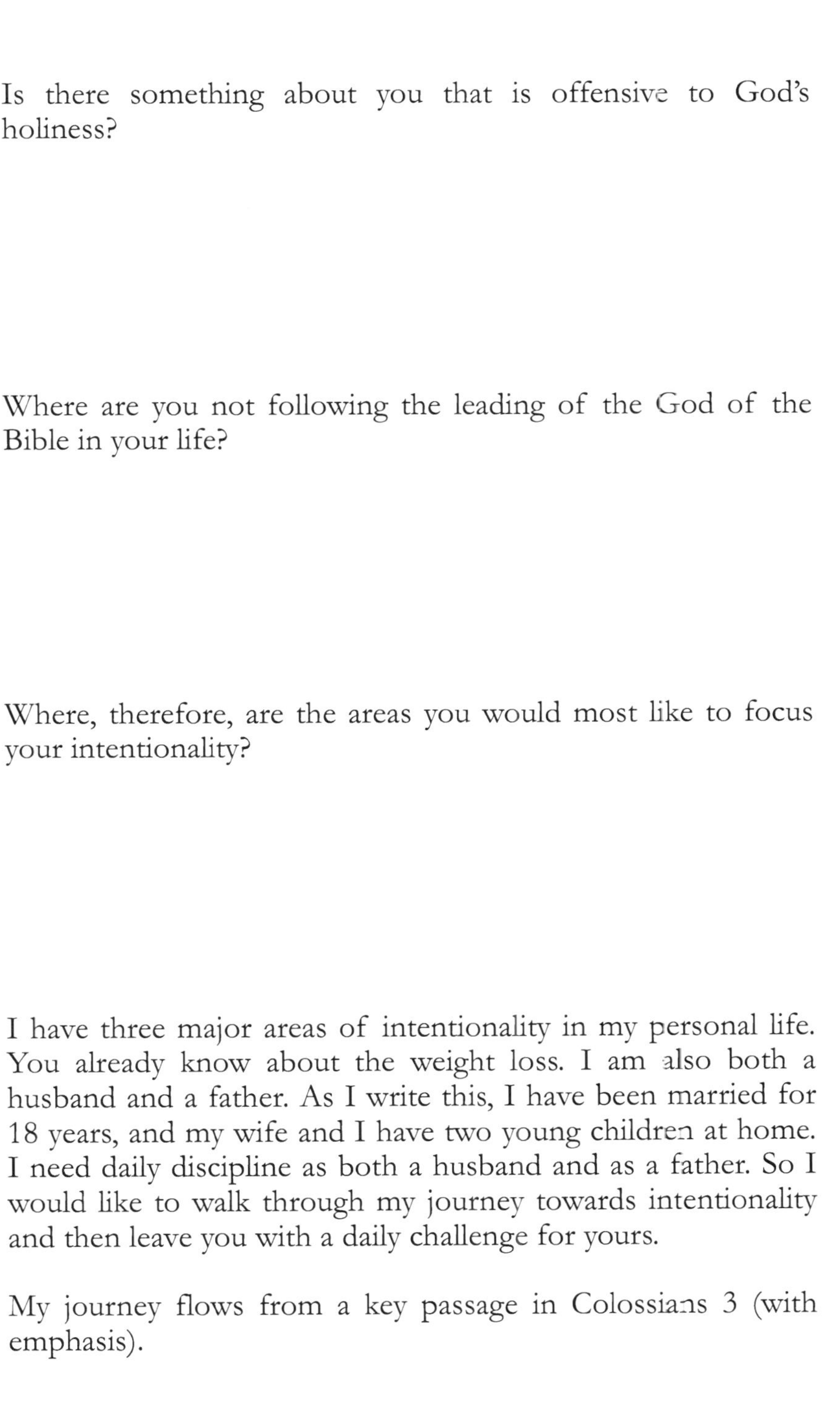

Is there something about you that is offensive to God's holiness?

Where are you not following the leading of the God of the Bible in your life?

Where, therefore, are the areas you would most like to focus your intentionality?

I have three major areas of intentionality in my personal life. You already know about the weight loss. I am also both a husband and a father. As I write this, I have been married for 18 years, and my wife and I have two young children at home. I need daily discipline as both a husband and as a father. So I would like to walk through my journey towards intentionality and then leave you with a daily challenge for yours.

My journey flows from a key passage in Colossians 3 (with emphasis).

Put to death therefore what is earthly in you: sexual immorality, impurity, passion, evil desire, and covetousness, which is idolatry. On account of these the wrath of God is coming. In these you too once walked, when you were living in them. But now you must put them all away: anger, wrath, malice, slander, and obscene talk from your mouth. Do not lie to one another, seeing that you have put off the old self with its practices and have put on the new self, which is being renewed in knowledge after the image of its Creator. (Colossians 3:5-10)

What helped me in my own journey was to make two lists. The first list contained what described the former me before Jesus changed my life. The second list contained what changed about my life because of Jesus. As the Gospel worked in and through my story, I asked myself what has described, or should describe, the new me?

When I go through these verses with others, I have them make those two lists for themselves. I hope you are reminded of the previous chapter of this book and those lists regarding fruit. There is selfish fruit on your branches that shouldn't be there and fruit that is not there that should be there. The old you before Christ shouldn't be the current you in Christ.

I now invite you to take the journey with Colossians 3 that I once and currently still travel. Think about your life before you became a committed follower of Jesus Christ.

What perspectives, attitudes, and actions once described you?

What has Jesus changed about you? What describes you in Christ now?

What would change about your daily life if you put off the old self and put on the new?

Many people talk about needing discipline. I know that I require discipline in my life. Any positive change in my life is because of living in a disciplined way. Think of intentionality as daily discipline. <u>Discipline is learned through consistent practice.</u>

When it came to weight loss, the only way I was going to make the Man Camp 50 pound goal was by daily taking off the old desires and putting on new ones. A cheesecake once taught me discipline. Let me illustrate.

We recently hosted a family Christmas party and a family member brought one of those big variety cheesecakes. Can you picture what they look like? This family member always brought this particular style of dessert and in this instance only a few pieces were eaten at the party. I knew right away that this cheesecake was going to impact my weight loss journey in two ways. First, I was raised not to throw food away. So I couldn't do that. And so I tried sending the cheesecake home with everyone I could. When that didn't work, I knew I was in trouble. I love pairing black coffee with desserts. Any other year I would have been celebrating the cheesecake. But I had made a promise to 200 guys! It was time for intentionality.

So rather than throwing it away, I made a plan. I allowed myself one piece a day as part of my routine. I adjusted my calories and my food choices to reflect this daily item, but I made it work. Those cheesecake pieces unbalanced my macronutrient levels, for not all calories are equal. I knew that I would have to adjust for this each day.

I usually wanted more than one piece of cheesecake. And so I went to war within my thought life. I directed my thoughts to allow for one piece of cheesecake a day. My discipline began with my self-talk. When I wanted a second piece later in the day, I had to remind myself of the boundary that I had set. I looked forward to getting up the next day and making that cup of coffee. I reserved my solitary piece of cheesecake for my Bible devotion time. I sought satisfaction and sufficiency in the Bible and with my sweet tooth! My intentional journey therefore motivated me. A cheesecake "taught" me weight loss discipline one daily slice at at time. But I also needed intentionality as a husband and as a father. Thankfully, God brought me through such a season.

The quarantine of 2020 was a frustrating time for many and a scary time for others. But for me it was a blessing as it gave me opportunities to work on my marriage and on my parenting. Like many of you reading this, my family was in the house together for most of each day. Thankfully, my wife and I each were able to work from home. Our children "attended" school on technological devices with apps and video conferencing. I'm firmly convinced that the children of that generation will look back at that season as "the good ole days." Dad and Mom were always home!

My friend and accountability partner would regularly challenge me with Ephesians 5:25, which reads *"Husbands, love your wives, as Christ loved the church and gave himself up for her."*

Was I loving my wife sacrificially? Was I daily giving myself up for her with my attitude? I was really struggling with this. I needed to be intentional in my marriage. I also entered into the stressful quarantine season an angry, impatient father. I could only get my children to listen to me if I raised my voice and yelled. My attitude was destructive to the climate of my home and I needed to be intentional about leading them in a different, more biblical direction.

With the help of a wonderful counselor, I began to own my sinful and selfish attitudes and put in good work regarding areas on which to focus. It is during this season that I ran across a few verses in Deuteronomy 12. These illustrate my perspective during quarantine.

You shall tear down their altars and dash in pieces their pillars and burn their Asherim with fire. You shall chop down the carved images of their gods and destroy their name out of that place. You shall not worship the LORD your God in that way. But you shall seek the place that the LORD your God will choose out of all your tribes to put his name and make his habitation there. There you shall go… (Deuteronomy 12:3-5)

Moses was commanding Israel to be intentional about tearing things down that were idolatrous and leading them astray. The nation was also to focus on the place where God had chosen. <u>I had things I needed to "tear down" about my attitude and selfishness. I also needed to focus on being the husband and father God had called me to be</u>. Just like with the putting off and putting on of Colossians 3, Deuteronomy 12 invited me to tear down and also to focus.

So I decided to maximize the quarantine season. Since we were always in the same house together, I decided to make little changes to my daily choices. I treated my home as an active science experiment. If I adjusted this attitude, what would result? If I instead responded to stress this other way, would it lead to change? I didn't think in those terms just yet, but I was focusing on being intentional.

I started asking my wife and kids for forgiveness the same day when I had gotten angry and yelled at them. I began tearing down my sarcastic responses. I was intentional about tearing down selfishness and focusing on humility. I focused my energies on washing the dishes each night before bed. Serving my wife was a necessary replacement for sarcasm and selfish arguing. I was putting off the old Joel and putting on the new. I was focusing on loving my wife sacrificially and leading my home with humility and service. I had failed at this for so long, but quarantine gave me the opportunity to be intentional!

Owning my issues is always the greatest intentional move I can make. Responding with humility and service was and is the leadership attitude I needed to show in my home. I will never forget one night when I had asked my son and daughter for forgiveness when I had lost my temper and angrily yelled at them for not listening to me. Joshua responded, "Of course, Daddy. I always forgive you."

That hit me directly in my heart. I wanted that very night to not only be a person who humbly asks for forgiveness, but also the kind of man who learns and starts intentionally living differently. I began to remind myself that though seeking forgiveness was good, not responding with sarcasm or anger in the first place was even better. I began to be intentional about being the type of husband and father that lived differently and made God-honoring choices to begin with.

And my wife and I saw results. Our marriage counseling sessions usually featured me owning what I had done wrong and practicing a better approach in the week to come. Our kids actually started asking us and each other for forgiveness when they had said or done something wrong. I was intentional about tearing down my selfishness and focusing on humility and service. And though we were still working on things daily, our home had started to become a new environment. My wife was intentional about things in her control and she partnered with me regarding tearing down and focusing. I like to think that after years of frustration and failure, we had utilized a time of worldwide fear and frustration to grow our marriage and parenting!

What needs to be "torn down" in your life? Think of attitudes, actions, and words.

Where are you needing to focus instead?

Ancient Israel needed to tear down those altars, otherwise they would be tempted to worship the idols there. You can't stay faithful to someone if you are giving your allegiance and love to someone else. Yahweh demands exclusivity. But they also needed to build the altar for God where he told them so they had a place to worship. They needed to intentionally break down and build up. These also serve as metaphors for their lives and ours. What needs to be torn down and what needs to be built up in your life? Be intentional.

Before we leave this chapter, let us look at the heart of intentionality, the heart of discipline. Proverbs 5 contained a command for the man tempted to stray.

Drink water from your own cistern, flowing water from your own well. (Proverbs 5:15)

Clearly the context here is a warning against adultery and adultery is always wrong. But we who face temptations of any kind know that intentionality and discipline are necessary in the battle. At the minimum, each of us faces the misguided cultural prompting to follow our hearts and to let our desires lead us around. So let's all take one interpretative step back and see the Proverbs 5 issue for what it really is—a matter of the heart. For such sins begin in the heart. What does discipline look like regarding the heart?

Discipline Learns To Rejoice

The man in the proverb was told to rejoice in his wife rather than going to another woman. And joy may need to be learned. There is something secure and lasting about a response of joy. This perspective comes through discipline and is clearly a work of the Holy Spirit in the Christian. Joy is a fruit of the Spirit (Galatians 5:22) and is to be the intended response grown in all situations (Philippians 4:4). Thus, the disciple learns to rejoice in all matters of trial in life (James 1:2-3). Rejoice in what you have and in the situation to which you have been led. Joy is always a response towards God.

Discipline Grows In Contentment

Contentment tells God that He is enough and what He has provided is also enough. It is far too tempting for many people to always be looking for something different or something more. Discipline grows in another direction and therefore looks to God instead of looking to the self. The self will never on its own be content. The selfish heart always seeks for more. Discipline denies the self and doesn't follow the selfish leadings of the heart.

Discipline Stops Looking Around

Enough already. You have two or three places you should look. Look "up" in the sense of gratitude and thanksgiving to how God has faithfully provided for you. Look outside of you in the sense of how you can be a blessing to others as you give glory to God. Look within and focus on how God has provided for you. Your daily response should be one that honors God. When we look around, we plant heart seeds of jealousy, envy, discontent, and bitterness.

Discipline Seeks The Only True Satisfaction

A lust is never satisfied. The thirst of selfishness is never quenched. So the seeking of these things will never pay out.

"But seek first the kingdom of God and his righteousness…" (Matthew 6:33)

The man in the proverb was seeking something different and something "more" than what he had. This was not good. True satisfaction is found only in seeking God and ultimately in God.

So time for a heart check. <u>If you despise growing in discipline then you are not responding as a disciple.</u> Discipline and disciple are basically the same English word. If you claim to follow Jesus, then you are a disciple. This doesn't have to be about sexual sin like in the chapter today. Each of us faces various temptations to be selfish. Drinking from your own cistern or well at its core is about satisfaction, contentment, and joy. Telling your thoughts and heart to stop looking around for the next, the newest, the other.

For me, this is truly a hard-knocks kind of learning proverb. I have to work on those four truths every day. Discipline never stops putting in the work. Especially when it comes to matters of the heart. <u>You affect your heart by disciplining your mind. You discipline your mind through self-talk</u>. Learning to thank God and being satisfied with that self-talk is better than saying you deserve more or are entitled to something other than what you currently have.

<u>Discipline is where intentionality meets the every day</u>. Where you are intentional is where you are disciplined. I went into

this year's Man Camp with a great report. Many guys remembered me and my big promise. They therefore asked me my number and how the year had gone. I shared that not only had I lost the 50 pounds and kept it off, but that I had lost 60!

It was a joy to write this chapter because it celebrates the intentional work of God. He makes discipline possible and then provides for my daily journey. My big three areas were ones where I had been a "functional hypocrite" for many years. So I trusted God, put in the work, and now have hope. <u>Intentionality and discipline are the soils where hope is grown and maintained</u>. And hope leads us to our next chapter.

CHAPTER 6

IN WHAT DO YOU HOPE?

Like cold water to a thirsty soul, so is good news from a far country. (Proverbs 25:25)

If you are like many people, when you are most thirsty only cold water will do. I recall many times working myself to exhaustion as I mowed the lawn in the summer heat. As I trudged back into the house I had only one thing on my mind. When I entered the kitchen I didn't reach for the gallon of milk or brew myself a cup of coffee. No, it was two quick glasses of water from the faucet. My wife will sometimes even send one of the kids outside with a glass of ice water if I am I the middle of the job. They marvel at Daddy chugging the entire glass in mere moments. It was what I needed. I was thirsty.

I also recall the lone season of college football I played. It was during the "hell week" practices in the hot August sun. I remember during those practices having the most unique of water breaks. The coaches had added many lengths of plastic pipe to the sprinkler system along one of the sidelines on the practice field. They then had drilled little holes along the pipes. When the water spigot was turned on, blessed arcs of water shot out from those tubes in such a manner that the entire team could drink at the same time. I remember being so thirsty that day that I didn't even remove my helmet to drink and simply allowed the water to reach me through my face mask!

Each of us has a soul that also thirsts. Some of us are struggling outwardly and long for peace, security, or comfort. We have relationships that are broken and we desire forgiveness or reconciliation. Some of us struggle inwardly and long for answers in the midst of our anxieties and fears. Many of us want to stop feeling the weight of bitterness or shame. Some of us long for the end of our pain and for our most pressing needs to be met.

Simply put, we thirst. We are sweat-soaked and exhausted from the pains of life and long to drink in refreshment and relief. When we are most depressed and anxious we are trapped on the path of self-focus. It can be very helpful to be still and to consider the world outside of our personal experiences. There is value in looking outside ourselves for some good news. I submit to you that your only true hope exists apart from yourself.

You may not feel like much is good in your corner of the world sometimes, but it is indeed refreshing to hear about hope in other places, that the God who can provide is indeed doing so! This is one of the many reasons churches support and partner with foreign missionaries. I always marvel at what God is doing in far off lands. I have myself personally set foot on five of the world's seven continents and through my journeys have seen God's faithful hand at work!

In this chapter, I want to introduce you to two men who represent some cold water for your thirsty soul. Unless you are reading this book in the Middle East, these men were from a faraway land and they lived many centuries ago. Both of these guys needed hope in the midst of their stories. So I invite you to think about where you find your hope. That's our sixth question on this journey.

But before we meet the first man, would you please take a moment and list the situations and struggles you currently face? Please jot down the difficult matters on your heart where you might feel hopeless or without answers.

[Jesus] also told this parable to some who trusted in themselves that they were righteous, and treated others with contempt: "Two men went up into the temple to pray, one a Pharisee and the other a tax collector. (Luke 18:9-10)

The first man I want to introduce to you is that tax collector in Jesus' parable. To help you to better grasp this character, let me describe to you a hypothetical scenario. Imagine there was a person in the county where you live who paid money to the government for the right to collect your property taxes. Sounds crazy, right? Now imagine that the authorities allowed him to charge whatever he thought he could get you and other homeowners to pay, and after submitting the tax payments was allowed to keep the rest for himself. This is how he made his millions.

How do you picture yourself feeling about this guy and the scam that he was running? That's how the people in Jesus' day viewed the tax collectors. And what made it worse was that these were Jewish people cheating their fellow Jewish neighbors to send that money to the hated Gentile Roman overlords. So not only were they seen as cheaters but also as political and ethnic traitors.

Jesus paired Mr. Traitor with a Pharisee. Do you have a person in your life who seems to be really religious and concerned about the things of God? Maybe they are always seen reading their Bible. They never miss a church service and always remember to have a donation to put in the plate. This person, no doubt, would be happy to talk about their favorite Scripture verses and are well read in theology. Picture this guy now walking into the temple that day with the tax collector to pray. We'll call the Pharisee Mr. Righteous. How do you think God would handle those prayers that day?

The purpose of Jesus' parable was to confront those who trusted that their own righteousness justified them before God. These were the kind of people who naturally looked down their nose at others "lesser" than them. Let's say you also went into the temple that day. You might have seen Mr. Righteous standing next to Mr. Traitor. If God was going to listen to anyone it certainly wasn't going to be the tax collector, right? Which of those two guys would you say had any hope of being good with God? It is most likely that the crowd around Jesus that day was thinking along those lines.

The Pharisee, standing by himself, prayed thus: 'God, I thank you that I am not like other men, extortioners, unjust, adulterers, or even like this tax collector. I fast twice a week; I give tithes of all that I get.' (Luke 18:11-12)

Ok, so Mr. Righteous was perhaps a little too cocky for our taste, but did he have a point? Many people might expect God to listen to their prayers if they had lived their lives doing all the proper things on the outside.

But the tax collector, standing far off, would not even lift up his eyes to heaven, but beat his breast, saying, 'God, be merciful to me, a sinner!' (Luke 18:13)

How do you feel reading that simple prayer? Maybe you appreciate the posture Mr. Traitor was taking before God. Perhaps you agree that he indeed was a sinner and therefore had no right to make any requests of God. Why would God listen to the prayer of someone like him? Surely, Mr. Righteous had more hope of God listening to him than Mr. Traitor! And that's when Jesus concluded the parable.

I tell you, this man [the tax collector] went down to his house justified, rather than the other. For everyone who exalts himself will be humbled, but the one who humbles himself will be exalted." (Luke 18:14)

Who has any hope of being justified before God? The humble sinner has more hope than the self-righteous religious person. Tax collectors and prostitutes repented in Jesus' day, but many Pharisees rejected him! Every time I read this parable of Jesus, the tax collector's prayer cuts me to the heart. I am that man. The only hope I ever have had has been the result of being humble before God and trusting in the mercy and grace only He can give. In terms of biblical hope for the sinner, that is what you face as well. No matter what your life looks like on the outside, you no doubt face sin and temptation on your inside.

There is hope in our stories! But before we get there, will you just take a moment and link your story to the two men Jesus described? What about the tax collector's attitude should be your response right now? Does anything with the Pharisee's approach to God describe yours? I invite you to write down any connections here.

Ponder this next verse and our two men for just a moment.

For godly grief produces a repentance that leads to salvation without regret, whereas worldly grief produces death. (2 Corinthians 7:10)

Paul had written the Corinthian Christians a previous letter that included pastoral admonishment and much correction. And he had just received word from Titus that the letter was received as intended. The church was grieving and humbled from the rebuke. They were earnest and afraid and wanting to repent from the evil ways they had slipped into.

And that was Paul's point. There is one type of grief that just makes you focus on yourself. It keeps you mired in your situation and drowning in your feelings. If you are anxious your fear is most likely at top level. If you are depressed, the story you are maintaining is most likely swamping you.

Worldly grief is something that only pulls you down deeper into the swamp. It offers no perspective or hope. The situation stinks and there seems little that can be done about it. Maybe you have lost a loved one and you feel stuck in your grief. Perhaps your divorce papers have just become finalized and you have begun to be bitter towards everyone. You might be facing something like unemployment or even infertility and those circumstances have you mired in feeling jealous or envious of others. Worldly grief causes you to feel emotionally trapped; the focus remains completely on yourself.

I recall one night of a recent vacation when that previous sentence clearly described me! It had been a one-hundred degree day in Florida. I had walked all over a theme park for many hours with my family. My two kids both had a rough day with their emotions. As I lay in bed that night, my mind began to wonder if the vacation was worth it, if I was a good parent, and if we should just go home. I couldn't even make a day at the "most magical place on earth" be a completely happy one! I was grieving all my expectations that had not come true. I was stuck. My depression was in high gear. Anxiety and shame stood at the ready. I felt both worthless and hopeless lying in that beautiful hotel bed and grieving over that day.

<u>It was a worldly grief, because it was focused on the stories I told myself</u>. There was no hope. There was no relief. I remember feeling thankful for my wife who listened to my

venting and whining. I recall being thankful for God who graciously allowed me to reset. My wife encouraged me saying that things would be ok. I wasn't the worst parent alive. It was still a great vacation, even if one night had me stuck in the quicksand of myself!

A godly grief instead focuses on Jesus. It is how the Holy Spirit works through a person's conscience to remind them of their sinful choices and their need to repent. To turn from themselves and to turn to God. That was part of my reset as I lie in bed after my hard day. I turned from myself and my stories and remembered God's faithfulness. I gave him my selfishness and prayed for a different perspective. So I guess that horrible night had some godly grief, too.

You may indeed be grieving many losses, but I encourage you to focus on Jesus as you do so. Therefore, you trust that God will provide another job or that your deceased loved one's destiny is God's business now. Your grief leads you to hope rather than to sink deeper within.

Like every Christian, I have at one time or another been faced with my sin and selfishness. Stuck on the "Joel" path and longing for something else. Godly grief is full of hope, because it leads to repentance and turning to Jesus, the only hope you could have. That repentance leads to salvation. It is how, in the famous Sermon on the Mount, Jesus could utter these words...

"Blessed are those who mourn, for they will be comforted." (Matthew 5:4)

You may feel stuck in your sin. I encourage you to see God at work with the grief you feel. Look for Him. The grief is there to lead you to repentance. Pay attention to your grief. It has a purpose. Godly grief leads to repentance, which you will never regret. Worldly grief leads you to focus on your regrets, which eventually feels like death. Hope comes to the intentional and to the repentant. I was never going to find any hope as I consistently focused on myself.

Now please take a moment and think about the hopeless situations you wrote down above. What changes about your stories if you adopt the humble repentance of the tax collector rather than the self-righteous pride of the Pharisee? Please write down those changes.

I want to close our time here with a wonderful focus from Romans. This is a great verse to have displayed in your home or office somewhere.

May the God of hope fill you with all joy and peace in believing, so that by the power of the Holy Spirit you may abound in hope. (Romans 15:13)

How does God bring hope to your day? First, He fills what needs filling. I know my days need that joy and peace that come from actually believing God. Mr. Traitor had hope because he trusted in God. He humbled himself and depended solely upon the grace and mercy that only God could provide. He had a profound emptiness that only God could fill. If Jesus gave us chapter two of Mr. Traitor's story, we might see how the tax collector's hope with God flowed into how he then treated others. When we have peace in our relationship with God the Gospel flows into our relationships with others. The vertical impacts the horizontal.

We, of course, want a second chapter of the Pharisee's story, as well. Was he even changed? Did he know what happened with that very tax collector that he despised? Did Mr. Righteous leave the temple feeling good with God? I know I have had moments where I faced my hypocrisy and humbled myself like Mr. Traitor. The only hope I ever have is because of the saving grace of Jesus. Yet far too often my story aligns itself with the true hypocrite, Mr. Righteous. I have to be intentional about the daily perspective and attitude of humility before God and others. Confession and humble repentance lead to change. Proclaiming my resume before God does not.

Let's land the plane with a proverb that was ahead of it's time!

He who loves wisdom makes his father glad, but a companion of prostitutes squanders his wealth. (Proverbs 29:3)

Have you ever wished you could think what Jesus was thinking? Well, guess what—this proverb was most likely on His mind when He told that famous parable of the Prodigal Son.

So let your mind travel to Jesus telling the parable of the Prodigal Son in Luke 15. Jesus' audience that day would have agreed with this proverb. The older son in the parable was literally living the perspective of Proverbs 29:3! All listening to Jesus were expecting the father in the story to treat the disrespectful, squandering son like he deserved.

But here's the thing: grace is never deserved. It is always God's love shown to the undeserving. So read how it all went down in Luke 15. Read the son's repentance moment and the father's response. It's the only time in Scripture where God "runs."

But when he came to himself, he said, 'How many of my father's hired servants have more than enough bread, but I perish here with hunger! I will arise and go to my father, and I will say to him, "Father, I have sinned against heaven and before you. I am no longer worthy to be called your son. Treat me as one of your hired servants."'

And he arose and came to his father. But while he was still a long way off, his father saw him and felt compassion, and ran and embraced him and kissed him. And the son said to him, 'Father, I have sinned against heaven and before you. I am no longer worthy to be called your son.'

But the father said to his servants, 'Bring quickly the best robe, and put it on him, and put a ring on his hand, and shoes on his feet. And bring the fattened calf and kill it, and let us eat and celebrate. For this my son was dead, and is alive again; he was lost, and is found.' And they began to celebrate. (Luke 15:17-24)

A son making wise choices makes a father glad. But a son repenting of his evil and returning to God, makes Dad CELEBRATE.

We need to see ourselves with the humility of the prodigal son. Mr. Traitor the tax collector was that son. I am that son. Grace is always undeserved. That first century crowd needed to hear that story told. This 21st century crowd does, too. Thank you, Jesus, for the hope that only You can provide. You are source of the greatest of hopes for hypocrites who humble themselves in repentance before You and plead for mercy. That wayward, lost son owned what he could about his situation and humbly went home trusting in his father's love. He had no idea that Dad was looking for him and running towards him! Biblical hope for the sinner follows that prodigal son's path back home!

We end our journey with pondering maybe the most important issue of all, the sovereignty of God. I invite you to pause right now to thank God for the hope that you have in and through Jesus.

CHAPTER 7

ARE YOU BITTER AGAINST GOD?

I am so glad you have made it to this point. For six chapters you have asked yourself difficult questions and have bravely peered into the crawlspace of your heart. If you're like me you have learned to see God at work in and through your story. But maybe the more you dig the bigger your gripe grows against God.

Let's examine matters theologically. God exists and you are not God. Therefore God alone is ultimately in charge of how history unfolds. And God only has a Plan A, for a Plan B implies that God needed correction or made a mistake. God therefore has a plan even for your story which has unfolded according to His sovereign plan.

Now let's imagine you are able to agree with those statements, can you see the opportunity to be bitter at God for His Plan A? I'm not looking to pick a fight between you and God, but take a moment and ponder God as King even over your story.

Are you angry with God regarding how your life has unfolded? What things do you find yourself holding against God?

Thank you for writing those down. I would now like to introduce you to a couple of Bible characters who each had a difficult life. Let's take some time and get to know both of their stories. The first is Naomi and she is the star of the short book of Ruth. Her story starts with pain.

So the two of them [Naomi and Ruth] went on until they came to Bethlehem. And when they came to Bethlehem, the whole town was stirred because of them. And the women said, 'Is this Naomi?' She said to them, 'Do not call me Naomi; call me Mara, for the Almighty has dealt very bitterly with me. I went away full, and the LORD has brought me back empty. Why call me Naomi, when the LORD has testified against me and the Almighty has brought calamity upon me?' (Ruth 1:19-21)

Naomi and her family had left her homeland to find food during a severe famine. During this stressful season, her husband and two adult sons died. We later find out in the story that the sons had earlier married women from their new home nation. At this point Naomi was left with three mouths to feed and zero of her breadwinning male family members. So she did the sensible thing and released her daughters-in-law—fellow widows—from any obligation to her. One woman accepted the release and the other instead clung to her. Naomi thus came back home. The town gossip mills were all astir as Naomi arrived with a foreign woman alongside her.

Naomi didn't have the easiest of situations. Think about the difficult situation or issue that you currently face. Maybe you described it up above. Perhaps you are depressed and angry at God. In her pain and loss, Naomi actually does two things.

First, Naomi changed her name to reflect her situation. Naomi meant "lovely" and Mara meant "bitter." She was bitter against God and she owned it to her core. The story that she told others was one that focused on her pain and her issues. Her identity was being a victim of the circumstances she had endured. Her life was therefore defined by her bitter anger. Her self-talk had kept her trapped.

Naomi not only changed her name, but she also found someone to blame. Yeah, I realize that previous sentence rhymes, but it might just be the thing you remember! Bitterness at God changes the stories we tell about God and about ourselves.

Naomi literally blamed God for her situation. Most of the bitter people I have met aren't as overt as Naomi was. They instead use their horrible situation as an excuse to not believe in the existence of God in the first place. "Why believe in the God who didn't solve my problems? Why would I believe and trust the God who did all this to me?"

Naomi had half of the matter right. The Bible does present God as both sovereign and in control. But Naomi thought God was working evil and not good for her. Since she found her life to be disappointing, the God she trusted must also be. And in her situation, many wouldn't blame her for feeling that way. Think back to the chapter about what stories you tell yourself. We tell ourselves stories about God, about others, and about ourselves. Read those above verses again, please. What story about God was she maintaining and how did it keep her locked down?

The second part of her story is Naomi's realization. When we last left Naomi, she was a bitter mess. She blamed God for her problems and maintained that story before the people of her hometown. Naomi had left with three men and now had returned home with one woman. Chapter 2 focuses on the actions of Ruth, the foreign daughter-in-law who went out looking for work.

So [Ruth] gleaned in the field until evening. Then she beat out what she had gleaned, and it was about an ephah of barley. And she took it up and went into the city. Her mother-in-law saw what she had gleaned. She also brought out and gave her what food she had left over after being satisfied. And her mother-in-law said to her, 'Where did you glean today? And where have you worked? Blessed be the man who took notice of you.' So she told her mother-in-law with whom she had worked and said, 'The man's name with whom I worked today is Boaz.'

And Naomi said to her daughter-in-law, 'May he be blessed by the LORD, whose kindness has not forsaken the living or the dead!' Naomi also said to her, 'The man is a close relative of ours, one of our redeemers.' And Ruth the Moabite said, 'Besides, he said to me, 'You shall keep close by my young men until they have finished all my harvest.' And Naomi said to Ruth, her daughter-in-law, 'It is good, my daughter, that you go out with his young women, lest in another field you be assaulted.' So she kept close to the young women of Boaz, gleaning until the end of the barley and wheat harvests. And she lived with her mother-in-law. (Ruth 2:17-23)

Ruth hatched a plan to glean in the fields. Her hard work would stand out in this story. It impressed Boaz and his crew and it provided for Naomi. So when Naomi saw Ruth come home with an abundance of grain, she wondered what had happened. How had Ruth come home with so much?

When Ruth shared the story about Boaz, Naomi's perspective immediately changed. She went from blaming God for her problems to declaring the praises of the God who shows kindness. What a transformation!

Depression comes down to the stories we tell ourselves. In Ruth Chapter One, Naomi's story was angry, accusing, and bitter. And now by Chapter Two it was grateful and with hope. What changed? Even in her pain she was able to see her situation with the eyes of faith. In her eyes the impossible had happened. Ruth just happened to wander to the field of the one man in Naomi's family who could have been a blessing. And that one man ended up not being like other men who might have taken advantage of an impressive young widow.

We give Naomi credit. She saw God at work immediately in her situation. Her story illustrates a wonderful lesson for us. She might not have been looking to see God at work, but she immediately recognized what only God could do. God was not her enemy, but was kind both to her and to the legacy of her dead sons and husband!

Then Naomi her mother-in-law said to her, 'My daughter, should I not seek rest for you, that it may be well with you? Is not Boaz our relative, with whose young women you were? See, he is winnowing barley tonight at the threshing floor. Wash therefore and anoint yourself, and put on your cloak and go down to the threshing floor, but do not make yourself known to the man until he has finished eating and drinking. But when he lies down, observe the place where he lies. Then go and uncover his feet and lie down, and he will tell you what to do.' And she replied, 'All that you say I will do.' (Ruth 3:1-5)

When I first begin to journey with people, they sometimes seem to be so stuck in their situations. They are buried beneath shame and guilt. The weight of depression is heavy.

Anxiety robs them of sleep. I always end our first session together with Biblical clarity and hope. What does God say in the Bible about their situation? How does the Bible uniquely address how God will work in their life? Once hope is established, we get to work.

Naomi had such a moment. In Chapter 1 she was buried beneath her situation. In Chapter 2 she had a moment of clarity and hope as she saw divine providence at work. So now in Chapter 3 Naomi herself got to work as she trusted in God.

Her plan did seem a little bit risqué as the threshing floor was known to have a reputation late at night, but I'm not questioning Naomi or Ruth's intentions here. Naomi had Ruth's future in mind and Ruth was respectful and obedient.

In depression, we first need to change the stories we tell ourselves. With Naomi, she changed the way she saw things from God had acted bad to God had acted good. And the second step is to get the focus off the self. Depression marinates in the self. It weighs upon us and depends upon harmful self-talk to maintain it. Naomi immediately shifted her focus from herself to Ruth. She made a plan to care for her daughter-in-law who was depending on her.

Naomi first shifted her story to seeing God at work in her life. Naomi then focused on serving others. These two steps are a great example for us!

So Boaz took Ruth, and she became his wife. And he went in to her, and the LORD gave her conception, and she bore a son. Then the women said to Naomi, 'Blessed be the LORD, who has not left you this day without a redeemer, and may his name be renowned in Israel! He shall be to you a restorer of life and a nourisher of your old age, for your daughter-in-law who loves you, who is more to you than seven sons, has given birth to him.' Then Naomi took the child and laid him on her lap and became his nurse. And the women of the neighborhood gave him a name, saying, 'A son has been born to Naomi.' They named him Obed. He was the father of Jesse, the father of David. (Ruth 4:13-17)

You have to love the book of Ruth. Such a sweet story of God's faithfulness. The greatest king of Israel, David, would have such amazing people in his lineage. He would have a man in Boaz who was a family redeemer who restored Naomi's losses and provided. David's family would also include Ruth, a foreign woman who left her comfort zones to faithfully cling to her mother-in-law and to her new God. And David would have in Naomi a great-great-grandmother, a woman who learned to trust God in the darkest season of her life and became an example to others.

Earlier in the book of Ruth, the women of the town got to witness Naomi's bitterness at God. And now they celebrated with her over God's faithfulness. This tells us that Naomi had maintained her new story, had continued to proclaim God's goodness to those around her. You could imagine Naomi being the talk of the town for all nine months of Boaz and Ruth's pregnancy.

<u>In all our situations, we should look for God's hand at work, trust in him, serve others, and then proclaim to others the new story we now tell ourselves of God's faithfulness</u>. Good friends will reinforce the new story in us. God is indeed faithful! Look how he has provided for you! The women of the town are evidence that Naomi in her depression had maintained her new hope. Naomi was redeemed from her bitter story. She had hope that was centered in God and illustrated by her son-in-law and baby grandson. Had Naomi continued to focus solely on herself and her story, she never would have found joy. She is one of my favorite Bible characters and I love introducing her to my bitter friends looking for hope.

Next let's look at Joseph's story from Genesis. Joseph had jealous brothers who sold him into slavery and then told their father that Joseph had been killed. By God's grace, Joseph ended up in Egypt as the steward running the house of a powerful official. The wife of that man took a fancy to Joseph and repeatedly tried to get him to sleep with her. One time when Joseph refused, the wife accused him of rape and Joseph ended up in jail for a crime he didn't commit.

While in prison Joseph rose to become the caretaker of all the inmates. Two of his fellow prisoners had dreams they couldn't interpret. Joseph relayed a favorable answer for one and an unfavorable answer to the other. Thus one man was restored to his job and the other was executed. And as the man was leaving to return to Pharaoh's side, Joseph simply asked the man to remember him.

Yet the chief cupbearer did not remember Joseph, but forgot him. (Genesis 40:23)

Chapter 41 tells us that two years later Pharaoh had a dream and then the cupbearer suddenly remembered about Joseph back in jail. Joseph was happy to help and since God had been with him though his story, Joseph succeeded. But let's not forget those two years! If you were Joseph, how would you have reacted? For many, those two years would have slow-cooked bitterness in their inner crockpots. <u>Bitterness is just anger and disappointment stewing for such a long time that it becomes your identity</u>.

Some of you reading this chapter are more like Naomi than Joseph. For as his story continued, Joseph would give no indication that he was bitter. That meant those two years were a time of faith and trust in God rather than anger and jealousy. Joseph gave evidence that he maintained a story of God being good rather than bad.

What grudges have you been simmering against God for quite some time? Maybe your life hasn't worked out they way you expected. Maybe people gave you their word and then never came through. Joseph would later be promoted to the second in command of the whole nation. And we don't read that he took revenge on that ridiculously forgetful cupbearer!

Joseph was called up and then immediately gave God glory. He wasn't mad at God or grumbling about God's plan. When you trust God, waiting becomes an opportunity to work those faith muscles. When you depend upon God, each new day is another opportunity to show that trust.

When you live with this perspective, your challenges become opportunities! I have friends who view their anxiety that way. They are grateful for what they go through because it teaches them to depend upon God. I view my depression through the same lens. I get to remind myself and repurpose my story every day that God is faithful and that He is with me and cares for me. He uses our stories for His glory! Joseph saw those two stressful years and trusted God. We know this because of how he talked about God before Pharaoh. His stress provided an opportunity for faith.

What are your stressful seasons providing an opportunity for in your story? What would you find God teaching you if you were paying attention?

God continued to be with Joseph and because of Joseph's leadership Egypt alone had food during a famine. Joseph's father sent his brothers to Egypt to buy food and the tension progressively mounted. Joseph eventually revealed himself to his brothers and then showed them grace rather than vengeance. Their father eventually died and the brothers feared that Joseph would have them murdered. Let's pick up the story at that moment.

His brothers also came and fell down before him and said, 'Behold, we are your servants.' But Joseph said to them, 'Do not fear, for am I in the place of God? ***As for you, you meant evil against me, but God meant it for good,*** *to bring it about that many people should be kept alive, as they are today. So do not fear; I will provide for you and your little ones.' Thus he comforted them and spoke kindly to them. (Genesis 50:18-21, with emphasis)*

Let's repeat those transcendent words: you meant it for evil, but God meant it for good. This is in my opinion a top 30 verse in the Bible...maybe top 20. This is the perspective of the person who sees life in God's hands. Joseph had already forgiven his brothers. And I think he did so when he started seeing God moving in his life in Potiphar's house or in prison or in Pharaoh's court. He had the faith that saw God moving the chess pieces in the background.

And once he recognized God was at work, he saw his situation in God's hands. All that had been done to him was accomplishing God's purposes. God was in control. Bitterness against those who wronged him was not possible. Joseph realized that all his suffering led to the survival of others. Bad should never come from good. <u>But, good can come from bad</u>. In an almost Christlike way, Joseph saw his suffering with that perspective.

Some of you reading this have gone through terrible circumstances or seasons. People have done rotten things to you or treated you horribly. You may even see yourself as a victim. It is tempting to feel justified in your struggle with bitterness. You may not feel like you are in a position to forgive the ones that wronged you. Others of you might be able to forgive your enemies, but just barely. I'm not sitting here in judgment of you. But just remember, Joseph had a huge, legitimate gripe against his enemies. And his enemies were even family!

But rather than seeing his situation as something to be avenged, he saw his life as in the hands of Almighty God. And he proclaimed that God can make good come from evil. This wouldn't be the last time God would do this. The greatest injustice of all time was sinless Jesus who died in a repentant sinner's place.

The greatest possible good came from the greatest possible injustice.

It takes a person of simple, but tremendous faith to be like Joseph. And for some, it takes decades to get there. It probably did for Joseph, too. Man meant it for evil, but God meant it for good.

<u>The path away from bitterness sees your life through God's eyes</u>. What has God taught you through your pain? How has He led you closer to him? How has He used your story for His glory? What was God accomplishing even through your times of suffering? Joseph's brother Judah was once the villain, but through humility and intentionality saw his story turn more into a hero.[10] Joseph was once a victim, but saw peace and joy as he showed grace and forgiveness to the undeserving.

I would like to conclude this chapter with the perspective that I have found on my own journey with God. One of the things I like to say is that life isn't always easy, but God is always faithful. But this statement has itself not come easily! I was diagnosed with multiple sclerosis my senior year of college. You might recall me mentioning this back in Chapter Two. I remember the disease robbing me of coordination, balance, and strength. All of this came as a surprise as I was in the prime of my physical life and nobody in my extended family had ever before faced this disease.

---

[10] In Genesis 37, Judah was the villain. In ch. 38, Judah was humbled by the Tamar episodes. By ch. 44, Judah was willing to take his brother's place in captivity. This caused Joseph to weep and reveal himself to his brothers. There is hope for any villain who humbly faces himself, owns his sins, and starts living biblically!

At college I immediately faced physical weakness and a dependance upon others for help. My fraternity brothers were my heroes in those earliest days. They cared for me the best they could. For some of them I was the only Christian in their lives. I remember them telling me that they had no idea why this God that I worshiped decided to give me MS. I have memories of some of them even getting angry at God because they knew I was suffering. But I tried to keep a smile on my face as best I could. Sometimes it felt like that was all I could do!

I have had this disease now for over half of my life. I have fallen and broken bones, felt numbness and dizziness, endured crippling pain and embarrassing balance issues. I haven't had full feeling in my hands since my 20s. I remember teaching myself to play guitar chords two different times (as my fingers allowed). I have had trouble expanding my chest muscles to breathe, experienced extreme motion sickness, and faced double-vision in each eye. Extreme temperatures rob me of my endurance and I feel hot flashes that keep me wanting to sit or sleep by a box fan!

I never remember feeling bitter with God. Right around the time of my diagnosis of MS in college, my pursuit of a medical career was coming to an end and I actually felt called to pastoral ministry. I didn't know then what God was doing in my story, but trusting God in my weakness made the most sense to me.[11] Others began to respond to my story that God was still faithful even though life wasn't always easy. Two of those fraternity brothers later came to me wanting to profess Christ as Savior. "We were all looking at how you handled life, JB. You didn't know it, but we were watching. This Jesus…I want what you have…" one of them told me.

Like Naomi, I needed to have eyes of faith to see God at

---

[11] I applied 2 Corinthians 12:9 here to my time of weakness. In context, Paul prayed for his torment to go away and God refused citing His sufficient grace. My hope then was that God looked strong as He sustained me in my weakness. That was God's response to Paul, as well.

work. A bitter Joel would have blamed God for giving MS to him. Instead I focused on trusting God for new strength to get through each day. Looking back, I learned through having MS to trust God. Trusting God is something I am really good at now. When I counsel people to trust God with the things they cannot control, that message comes from over 20 years of journeying with MS. I want my story to give God glory and trusting God as my strength in the middle of my weakness surely does so!

Joseph saw God at work in his life even though he endured so much. My wife Jennifer and I have experienced the loss of children. Our first baby, our sweet Esther, survived outside of the womb for about 15 minutes. There is only one date on her grave marker. Our second baby, Lily, miscarried from an ectopic pregnancy that almost killed Jen. We are grateful to God for our strong Joshua, the baby that we finally got to take home. Next came the twins, Julia and Grace. Gracie died around week 28 in the womb, and sweet Julia is our joy. My wife to this day is my hero. I am so grateful for her and am honored to journey alongside her.

Jen and I still trusted God even as we had to say goodbye to three of our five children. You might remember me mentioning these losses also back in Chapter Two. We look forward to our welcoming party in Heaven. Those three babies never would learn to talk. I like to imagine the first words they will ever say to me will be, "Hi Daddy, here is our friend Jesus!" They never cried. They never will.

Joseph didn't grow bitter at his situation. As I read his story I imagine a more bitter person saying, "Again, God? Seriously? How much more are you going to send my way!"

I am grateful for God's faithfulness to me. He gave me the strength and faithfulness to endure in such a manner that never said those words. As people hear my story today many have told me they are shocked at how much I have had to to endure. First there was the MS and now the loss of children. But by God's grace, this is not where I go in my own thoughts.

Bitterness robs you of the opportunity to find joy in how God has written your story. Since God only has a Plan A, trust that God knows what He is doing. He is both sovereignly God and blessedly good.

I've had to face that reality and maintain that perspective as I looked into the crawlspace of my own heart. Your journey through this book might have revealed struggles that you currently are facing. Whatever those struggles may be, please know that there is still time to be a transformed Naomi who recognizes God at work in your story. You still have the opportunity to respond like Joseph who saw God's plan even through his pain. Bitterness doesn't have to be your story either. Don't give up! I invite you to join me in trusting God. Look for God's hand at work in your story, my friends.

Life sometimes really stinks, but God is always faithful!

CONCLUSION

WHY A CRAWLSPACE?

"Can we sit at the bar?"

I had wanted to take my wife Jennifer out for dinner on our anniversary. So I had made the babysitting plans with Grandma and Papa. I even offered any restaurant that Jen preferred. I remember her choosing a "barbecue and blues" themed place she knew was my favorite. The restaurant only took walk-ins and thus we were unable to make a reservation. Therefore, after dropping off the kids, we had made our way there hoping for the best regarding a table. We soon found out that there was a wait of over an hour to be seated.

My mind had started racing as to what other eating options we might have chosen. *Would they have all had a similar wait? Would our anniversary date now be ruined? How were we going to get back and get the kids at a reasonable time?* You have already met this side of me from my vacation overreaction back in Chapter Six! Thankfully, Jen interrupted my self-centered internal conversation with the above question I quoted. "Can we sit at the bar?"

They seated us at the restaurant bar immediately and we were able to order as normal off of the menu. I was worried that not sitting at a table would have seemed like a lesser anniversary meal and been seen as less romantic. But little did I know that Jen would be in her element!

She connected right away with the younger woman who was tending the bar, listening to what was going on in her life and offering sympathetic comments. Jen also interacted with the male bartender and rejoiced at the good news he shared about a new baby in his extended family arriving soon.

The whole bar area quickly learned that it was our anniversary and Jen even wove into our story that one of our earliest dates almost twenty years ago involved having barbecue at another location in their restaurant chain. At hearing that, the entire bar area fell in love with us! It ended up being the perfect anniversary meal. In fact, I jokingly called our seventeenth year the barbecue sauce anniversary!

I found sitting at the bar with Jen that night to be the most romantic date and an anniversary I will never forget. And I simply LOVE how the meal ended. I remember as I was paying the bill Jen encouraging me to leave a generous tip. As the last people were saying goodbye to us, we were finally asked how we met.

"We met at seminary."

"Yeah, I'm a pastor and she's a chaplain."

The young man cleaning the bar area smiled and said, "Well, praise Jesus, then!"

Indeed. You might recall me asking the question about fruit back in Chapter Four. If you belong to Jesus, you daily display the fruit of the Spirit in your life. Those fruits are love, joy, peace, patience, kindness, goodness, faithfulness, gentleness, and self-control.

I'm so glad that I journey with a wife that showed peace, gentleness and faithfulness during what could have been a stressful evening. Love and joy were obviously present. Jen showed kindness to the woman tending the bar. My wife even used our story for goodness as she cared for others.

Our story, in fact, seemed to have had a wholesome goodness to it. We found that both workers and customers wanted to smile with the pastor and his wife celebrating their wedding anniversary at the bar! And as for me, I got the remaining fruit. The once stressful evening was an opportunity for me to grow in patience and self-control.

I just wanted to take a moment in this final bonus chapter to thank you for journeying with me. It's possible that this book was given to you by someone, or you are working through these questions with a trusted friend or two. You might have even been asking a key question of yourself this whole time.

Why Does Your Heart Even Have A Crawlspace?

I wanted to share with you two principles from the following verses that I hope will bring our journey to a close.

Count it all joy, my brothers, when you meet trials of various kinds, for you know that the testing of your faith produces steadfastness. And let steadfastness have its full effect, that you may be perfect and complete, lacking in nothing. (James 1:2-4)

It is in the crawlspace of my heart where God tests my faith.

As my faith is tested with each new season or trial, God is growing steadfastness in me. That Greek word can also be translated "endurance." God uses each trial to strengthen my faith, to keep me trusting Him, to endure by not giving up! Like a bright flashlight in a dark room, trust in God shines strongest in seasons of difficulty. As I ask myself the seven questions of this book, God is at work in my crawlspace teaching me to live my faith in both trust and obedience.

It is in the crawlspace of my heart where God perfects and completes what is lacking in me.

Back in my undergraduate college years I was living life as a functional hypocrite. I outwardly claimed faith in Christ, but inwardly was stuck in addictions and selfishness. I lacked discipline and dedication to Jesus in my crawlspace. It was in this season that I was diagnosed with MS and began the journey of understanding what it meant to depend upon Jesus daily. I had just finished a season of college football and had never been physically stronger. God then taught me humility by leading me through times of physical weakness.

I also later joyfully pastored a small church for 10 years, but eventually witnessed its slow, steady decline. My crawlspace was full of frustration and envy as I struggled with the plans of God and my future as a pastor with a young family. God continued to grow in me dependence and faith. I never gave up hope in God's plan even though the budgets grew leaner and the attendance numbers continued to decline. In the midst of my depression, God reinforced my faith with the promise from Galatians 6:9 that we will one day reap a harvest if we don't give up, so keep doing good!

I got needed help in my selfish journey regarding my addiction. Through the guidance of my wife, I saw biblical counselors and began attending Celebrate Recovery.[12] I now celebrate ten years of sobriety and I journey with others who regularly face their own rock-bottom helplessness. <u>God did an amazing work in my crawlspace that changed the course of my life and gave me a story of hope and deliverance</u>!

And this is eternal life, that they know you, the only true God, and Jesus Christ whom you have sent. (John 17:3)

<u>The great relationship goal of this life is to know Jesus</u>. Throughout the pages of this book you have been challenged

---

12 https://celebraterecovery.com

to stop certain behaviors or attitudes and to start others. But change in the Christian life is not something that is simply reduced to behavior management. Rather, we seek to change because of Jesus and our relationship with Jesus.

As we read the Bible, the Holy Spirit goes to work in the crawlspaces of our hearts and brings the conviction and encouragement we require. We change because God both leads us to change and guides the process of change. He progressively makes each believer less like the former self and more like Jesus.

The very wife I celebrated on our "barbecue anniversary" was and continues to be a major blessing to me regarding my crawlspace issues! I wake up each morning with the word *gratitude* on my mind. I am grateful for my wife and how God uses her. I am grateful for my Jesus and I am grateful for the wife He has given me. Let me share one final story.

In the final days of writing this book, my wife and I suffered an early first-trimester miscarriage. We were so grateful to God for allowing us to be pregnant one final time, and we had so much hope for another child after our previous losses. But it was God's will for us to say goodbye to now four of our six children. Eternal life matters to Jen and me because it is in eternity when we will see those four precious children again. With this baby we hadn't yet gotten too far in the naming process. We had been calling this dear one Jelly Bean.

The Gospel message matters to us because it offers that tremendous hope. Knowing Jesus matters because that relationship leads to eternal life. One day, Jen and I will see our precious Esther, our Lily, our Grace, and now our Jelly Bean. As I write these words with tears in my eyes I give perspective to their short lives. Our daily prayer is that our Joshua and our Julia will know Jesus and follow Him all the days of their lives. They may have to at times peer into their own crawlspaces, but the journey will be worth it!

This is why we dig deep into the crawlspaces of our hearts. Eternity matters, and that eternity is only possible through Jesus. I simply cannot give Him glory if I neglect the darkest, most hypocritical parts of my being! That is your story too, my friend. This is why you have made it this far and have done the difficult but necessary work in the crawlspace of your heart.

I thank you for thoughtfully reading this book. I pray that each chapter not only challenged you, but also brought encouragement. The journey peering into the crawlspace of your heart may have hurt. It hurt when I squeezed my wide shoulders into that original crawlspace searching for gnats. But that journey led to answers and therefore brought hope. I pray that these pages have sparked conversations and furthered commitments as you also found hope. As God has gotten glory through the changes in me, may He be further glorified by the heart changes in you.

ACKNOWLEDGMENTS

A special thank you to Eric and Sara for their friendship and help.

I am grateful and thankful for Jamie, Maddie, and Ally's key assistance.

Scott Z, thank you for putting me on the path of biblical counseling.

Brian, Junior, Jordan, Mick, Mike, and Scott O, I am thankful for your friendship!

Terry, the Edgy Elder, you have been such a blessing to me!

ABOUT THE AUTHOR

Joel is an ACBC certified biblical counselor who has served in pastoral ministry for over 20 years. He serves as Care Pastor of The Bridge Community Church, a multi-site church in the Chicago, IL area. Joel writes a daily Bible blog devotional, and hosts a podcast called "Masterclass Theology." For more information, or to follow the daily content, scan the QR code below or go to www.joelmbradshaw.com.

Made in the USA
Middletown, DE
05 September 2024